Discovering You

First Steps for Developing Your Emotional Intelligence

Rebecca Haskett
and
David Neidert

WESTBOW
PRESS®
A DIVISION OF THOMAS NELSON
& ZONDERVAN

This book is a work of non-fiction. Unless otherwise noted, the author and the publisher make
no explicit guarantees as to the accuracy of the information contained in this book and in
some cases, names of people and places have been altered to protect their privacy.

WestBow Press books may be ordered through booksellers or by contacting:

WestBow Press
A Division of Thomas Nelson & Zondervan
1663 Liberty Drive
Bloomington, IN 47403
www.westbowpress.com
1 (866) 928-1240

Because of the dynamic nature of the Internet, any web addresses or links contained in this
book may have changed since publication and may no longer be valid. The views expressed
in this work are solely those of the author and do not necessarily reflect the views of
the publisher, and the publisher hereby disclaims any responsibility for them.

Any people depicted in stock imagery provided by Thinkstock are models,
and such images are being used for illustrative purposes only.
Certain stock imagery © Thinkstock.

Scriptures taken from the Holy Bible, New International Version®, NIV®. Copyright © 1973,
1978, 1984, 2011 by Biblica, Inc.™ Used by permission of Zondervan. All rights reserved
worldwide. www.zondervan.com The "NIV" and "New International Version" are trademarks
registered in the United States Patent and Trademark Office by Biblica, Inc.™

ISBN: 978-1-5127-5390-5 (sc)
ISBN: 978-1-5127-5389-9 (e)

Library of Congress Control Number: 2016913398

Print information available on the last page.

WestBow Press rev. date: 08/23/2016

CONTENTS

FOREWORD

A 2004 seminar set the stage for this collaborative work that now spans a decade. Becky had completed her doctorate with her dissertation focused in the area of Emotional Intelligence (EI). David, in the audience, had also been contemplating EI but through academic lenses of biblical ancient wisdom and Christian theology. The growing EI research Becky shared during this Anderson University sponsored seminar, along with her personal story of transformation and career change based on increased self-discovery and awareness, became the catalyst for *Discovering You*.

We are from different backgrounds. Becky comes to her teaching role from the business world by way of corporate finance and strategic planning. David came to his university assignment from a Christian theology, biblical studies, and human development background with stints in business management and human resources.

An e-mail about getting together for kicking around our common interest was all it took. A few subsequent meetings unfolded an agreement that we could combine our unique EI perspectives for helping others discover their mission and purpose, all with the hope that people would find a clear process for discovering well-being in life, both as human beings and believers in Jesus Christ. As our discussions continued, we both saw how this project related to our own personal mission statements: (David's) *Inviting people to be and do good* and (Becky's) *Encouraging and assisting others in discovering their calling*. Both of these mission statements are about discovery and choices—detecting how to understand our calling in life and applying that knowledge to our relationships and how we act each day. Both of these mission statements also sit firmly on our own personal belief in Jesus Christ and our belief that he invites us to do good, live in fellowship with each other, and experience abundant life (Acts 10:38; 1 John 1:7; John 10:10).[1]

The title of this book, *Discovering You*, took shape over many years of discussion and reflection as we envisioned people using this material to begin a transformation through the renewal of their minds and hearts (Rom 12:1-2). The decision to utilize this format came after spending hours in the rows of leadership and self-help books at a few major booksellers. Almost every EI book offered explanations and provided convincing examples highlighting the importance of the concept but did not provide the reader with a roadmap to guide them in discerning and developing their own EI. We wanted our work to assist people in their discovery and transformation by creating exercises and activities that would help a person take responsibility for living their life with purpose.

We wish to thank many people for their participation in this project. First, we thank Anderson University, a place of "Academic and Christian Discovery," for providing space for us to come together. We are grateful for this school and its openness to collegiality, partnerships, and the pursuit of new ideas within a context of Christian discovery. We give special thanks to our families, where we have found lessons of transformation and faith honed and shaped. Thanks to Ted, Matt, Laura, Kristin, Jeremy, Sarah, Rick, and my parents (Becky's family) and Rhonda, Sarah, Damon, David, Caitlin, Mariah, Phoenix, Genesis, and Beau (David's family) for keeping us honest and providing the laboratory for learning how to become what we were intended to be.

We are also grateful to the faith communities that shape us weekly. For Becky, First Nazarene has permitted her to hear from others concerning editorial insights valuable to this book. David weekly teaches Ambassadorship 101 at South Meridian Church of God, where participants work together through Scripture for spiritual growth. Both believing communities nurture and sustain us for our vocational and community work.

University students and seminar participants from around the country have been instrumental in the research and activities contained in this material. These individuals have experimented with all the exercises we include and found them extremely useful. Thus, these exercises have been refined and sharpened through regular feedback and use, *so we know they work, if given a chance.* Thanks to the thousands who have helped us see our way in developing materials that assist individuals in personal reflection, self-awareness, and transformation.

Before you move beyond these pages to the core of the book, we want to extend a personal invitation: *We invite you not to skip the endnotes.* As authors, teachers, and practitioners in the area of EI and personal mission, we are continually learning more about these important topics. We have revised this book numerous times since its inception in 2005 to reflect our ongoing research, experiences, and spiritual growth. We have incorporated updated insights where appropriate in the body of the book, while providing more in-depth reflection or support in the endnotes. You will gain deeper appreciation for this topic by browsing through the endnotes, as well as reading some of the books we recommend.

As we come to the close of the foreword, we want to give thanks to God for his gift of this material and the opportunity for Becky and David to work together. We both believe our discernment and guidance comes through Jesus Christ, as our Lord and Savior. We prayed regularly for understanding as we labored over what to provide in this book over the past decade. We believe the Holy Spirit guided each step in our collaboration as we wrote what he placed on our hearts. We also are grateful that God helped us to understand how we are co-partners in his transformation of our lives. God invites us to take off our old nature and put on new in our obedience and service to him (Eph 4:20-24). We can only take off and put on new spiritual clothing as we understand our nature through awareness and what we learn (Eph 4:22). God has done such a work in us; we are pleased to share our own journeys through this book all to the glory of God. We are in full agreement with Peter Scazzero when he states, "Success as a follower of Jesus is to become the person God has called you to become and to do what God has called you to do."[2] There is no greater worship (Rom 12:1).

We are excited to offer you the opportunity, in this written format, to join those who have discovered new insights about themselves and made changes in how they live because of it. Blessings to you as you begin this journey of a lifetime.

Rebecca Haskett
David Neidert

Anderson, Indiana
2016

INTRODUCTION

There has been a growing interest in the topic of EI since the release of the bestseller *Emotional Intelligence: Why It Can Matter More Than IQ* by Daniel Goleman (1995). From personal reflection to corporate training sessions, EI is now considered to be a key factor in living and working well. At its core, EI is showing that managing your emotions is an important aspect for fulfilling your purpose in life and developing effective relationships. Peter Scazzero, author of *The Emotionally Healthy Leader* (2015), echoes this statement by noting that emotional health is most evident in one's closest relationships as experienced with a spouse, family or friends.[1]

Goleman's book sparked research that is demonstrating how EI is essential for many facets of life, including obtaining and maintaining a job. "Perfect" job applicants have the qualities of effective communication skills, honesty, interpersonal skills, teamwork, and motivation, which are all at the heart of EI.[2]

What is also interesting is that longevity studies point us to the reality that successful aging hinges on EI components (as measured by EQ).[3] George Vaillant's Harvard University Longevity Study of 824 people from childhood to death demonstrates that among six factors, strong EI early in life is a predictor of successful and well-adaptive life during the aging process.[4] Thus, a preponderance of research from many areas suggests that, unlike IQ, individuals can improve their levels of EI by identifying their personal areas of strength and weakness, and then going through a process of emotional learning.[5]

Discovering You as a Starting Point

Discovering You provides a framework for increasing your self-awareness, which is the foundation for developing your EI. We believe over the course of using this book, individuals will discover their strengths and weaknesses and determine how they will utilize this understanding for developing their EI.

We know individuals can improve their EI competencies and discover their purpose in life through the many years of testing the material in this book. Additionally, we have listened to personal stories of renewed lives by those who have utilized its process. This workbook contains unsolicited testimonials of personal change when a person is willing to test his or her self-perceptions against others, learn from their experiences, insights, and wisdom, and work to become who they were created and meant to be.[6] This deep change comes through a process that begins by taking time for understanding and then developing our EI. Is it risky business? Definitely. Is it worth the risk? We believe categorically, yes!

You have a choice of whether you experience meaning and purpose to your earthly existence or feel a thread of regret or uncertainty as you age, never fully becoming what God created you to be. You can play life safe, relying on your smarts to get you through, all the while never fully developing purposeful relationships or living as fully as you might. However, we know you can experience well-being both physically and spiritually and maintain effective relationships, if you choose to invest time in this process of discovery and transformation.

Personal growth is based on motivation, openness to God, courage to foster a realistic self-perception, and the choices that go with these qualities. Lasting change can come as you work through the steps that follow. It is worth the adventure.

Discovering You offers a method for beginning a personal journey that may ultimately lead to living the purpose you were created by God to live. We believe every person has a purpose, but with the overwhelming voices and choices clamoring for our attention, that purpose can be difficult to identify. It is our belief that *Discovering You* can help a person identify and clarify their *Best-self* (the person they are called to become and would like to be). Part of this discovery, however, also requires evaluating who we are now by identifying who we are currently in life (our *Today-self*).[7]

This work is not for us alone. This journey is important so that an individual might understand and manage their personal emotions, enabling them to improve personal health, live with a sense of happiness, and cultivate relationships that are effective and fulfilling. Ultimately, the journey can help you hear what God has called you to become and do as his steward during your life.

This Is a Working Book, So Let's Work

This book's design is intentional because we are convinced it is important to think about EI from the start. The reflection exercise that follows provides you an opportunity for gauging where you are at this moment of your life. It is not scientific by any means, but if you are honest with yourself, you might establish a sense of a starting place for using this book as a way of moving from your present *Today-self* to the image of the *Best-self*.[8]

Reflect on the statements below. Honestly respond to your current feelings or actions.	Strongly Agree	Agree	Neutral	Disagree	Strongly Disagree
I am experiencing disharmony or internal turmoil—I know that something is not right about my life, but I do not have the skills to resolve it.					
I know there is more to me, but I do not know how to live to my full potential or what God desires.					
I am faced with many choices/possibilities but lack self-awareness for making the best choices (college major, job, relationships, etc.).					
I have feelings of hopelessness or fearfulness.					
I have a pessimistic attitude about life.					
I am feeling overwhelmed, which leads me toward giving up on my hopes and dreams.					
I feel stuck in a rut.					
I feel the need to meet other's expectations.					
I have behaviors I cannot stop, even though I have tried.					
I constantly use negative self-talk.					
I am living the life I want to live.					
I am experiencing personal fulfillment or satisfaction in my personal and professional life.					
I am living a purposeful life; I am following what I believe God has invited me to do.					
I feel I have the tools to resolve life's struggles when they come my way.					
I am experiencing periods of flow in my work.					

Reflect on the statements below. Honestly respond to your current feelings or actions.	Strongly Agree	Agree	Neutral	Disagree	Strongly Disagree
I am fully engaged in life and relationships.					
I am optimistic and hopeful.					
I enjoy others or connect well with them.					
I am anxious about the next season of my life and what it will or will not offer.					

You may already possess a high level of self-awareness about a variety of emotions listed in the assessment and are motivated toward pursuing your life goals and hopes. Additionally, you may also be equipped for assisting others by further developing empathy, relationship skills, and encouraging others to join you in ongoing learning for creating and sustaining EI. If, however, the assessment made you aware you are not where you hope, desire, or believe God might lead you, we know the remainder of this book will guide you through a transformation to stronger EI skills, well-being in life, and relationships that are more effective. We affirm Peter Scazzero's steps to emotional health[9]: (1) we become aware of something, (2) we ponder it, and (3) we value it. Scazzero continues with two additional steps—changing one's behavior and actions, and owning it—but he acknowledges that most people never get past becoming aware of something (step 1).[10] We hope you will move through all five steps and not permit reading *Discovering You* to be a novel yet fruitless exercise of the mind.

As we have stated from the beginning, possessing effective EI skills benefits our lives and influences other people's lives as well. It is useful to complete an Emotional Quotient (EQ) assessment of your own EI skills and to also invite feedback from others. Take a moment to consider some drawbacks of below-average EQ when compared with the benefits of an above-average EQ.

Drawbacks of below-average EQ
- lack of self-awareness
- defensiveness—not open to constructive feedback
- behavior issues from feelings of frustration, lack of respect, etc.
- behavior stemming from unmet needs of acceptance, respect, etc.

- lack of empathy—lacking sensitivity to feelings of others
- using others to fill unmet emotional needs
- blaming others for one's own feelings
- letting feelings buildup and then blow up
- inflexibility
- avoiding responsibility
- poor listening habits

Benefits of above-average EQ[11]
- being a better learner—negative emotions inhibit learning
- fewer behavioral problems, less violent, less self-destructive behaviors
- ability to resist peer pressure and delay gratification
- more friends
- happier/more optimistic/hopeful—benefits of laughing
- healthier—improved immune system, reducing cancer, heart disease, etc.
- more "successful"
- expressing feelings in three word sentences, like "I feel _____." Easily understood by others[12]
- better able to read nonverbal cues displayed by others

Take a moment to reflect. Which group best describes you at this moment? While you might categorize yourself in one group over the other, *where would those who know you best place you? How would they describe you to someone else who does not know you? What adjectives would they utilize if they honestly talked about you with a mutual acquaintance?*

Being classified in the group demonstrating above average EQ is something we all desire. Yet we might not be where we hope or intend to be, unless we increase our self-awareness by spending some time thinking through our current behaviors and how others might view us. Whether above average or below in EQ, each group does have its effects on our own lives and the lives of others.

Our Invitation to You

Now that you have a sense of how EI can affect our lives and others, we invite you to take this journey toward transformation by first becoming acquainted with the background and research on the concept of EI. Why should you undertake such an arduous trek of discovery without comprehending the reason for its importance? Why should you take our word this is an investment worth every step?

We will explore the components of EI in the first section. The following pages will help you see why this process is essential in renewing your mind and heart with the ultimate reward of more effective relationships and living abundantly in Christ. There is a reason. There is a why. We trust the pages ahead might convert any skepticism you harbor to eagerness for the task.

Exploring Emotional Intelligence

What Is It and Why Is It Important?

"In the fields I have studied, emotional intelligence is much more powerful than IQ in determining who emerges as a leader. IQ is a threshold competence. You need it, but it doesn't make you a star. Emotional intelligence can."

Warren Bennis (1925-2014)
Scholar on leadership and business author

Have you ever wondered why some individuals lead contented and joyful lives, even when the circumstances of life seem to be against them? Instinctively, you may have suspected factors other than IQ contribute to their outlook, perceived success, career achievements, contented relationships, and an overall sense of physical and spiritual well-being. In the past decade, a growing body of research continues to support the evidence that EI is an important factor leading to a brighter outlook on life and healthier relationships.[1]

EI and Its Importance

EI involves becoming aware of and managing your own emotions.[2] This is not just for self-interest or gratification but also for developing effective relationships and living fully as an ambassador of Christ by seeking to understand, work well with, and serve others. As Scazzero observes, it is "operating emotionally and spiritually full...an overflowing life *with* God sufficient to sustain (one's) 'doing' *for* God."[3]

The following table provides a summary of the EI competencies[4] identified by two of the leading EQ assessments (i.e., the Emotional Competency Inventory, or ECI, by Daniel Goleman[5] and the Bar-On Emotional Quotient Inventory, or EQ-I, by Reuven Bar-On[6]).

Emotional Intelligence Competencies

INTRAPERSONAL/Personal Competencies	
SELF-AWARENESS	**IDENTIFIED THROUGH**
Understanding your emotions and personal strengths and weaknesses; accurately perceiving emotions as they happen.	Self-regard/confidence, self-actualization, self-assessment.
SELF-MANAGEMENT	
Effectively managing your own emotions, feelings, and resulting behavior; using awareness to direct your behavior.	Self-control, adaptability/flexibility, trustworthiness, impulse control, mood/optimism/happiness, stress mgt., conscientiousness, initiative/drive.
INTERPERSONAL/Social Competencies	
SOCIAL-AWARENESS	**IDENTIFIED THROUGH**
Understanding what others are saying and feeling and why they feel and act as they do.	Empathy, social responsibility/service orientation, organizational awareness/politics.
SOCIAL-SKILLS	
Effectively relating to and working with others; using your awareness to manage interactions.	Sustained relationships, communication, coaching/developing others, leadership, influence, change catalyst, conflict management, teamwork, assertiveness.

While we will focus in these pages specifically on the need for developing and living out our EI competencies, we will first explore where EI fits in the overall research and paradigm of multiple intelligences.

By this point in your life, you have likely encountered a person with a high level of cognitive intelligence (IQ) who is seemingly incapable of relating to other people with any civility or tact. Western culture identifies the intelligent person as having a high IQ. Western society places high value and esteem on those who rank in the upper ranges of IQ scoring, with genius groups having their own societies and organizations from which most of us are excluded.

This, however, is only one measure of being *wholly* intelligent. While a person may be considered intelligent in solving math problems or expounding world facts, they may be perceived or behave as unintelligent when it comes to relationships, the arts, athletics, or even how they communicate what they have cognitively catalogued. How, then, do we define what it means to be intelligent, and more specifically, what are the variety of ways human beings are intelligent beyond IQ?

We have come to understand over these past three decades that human beings have multiple intelligences, i.e., multiple capacities for understanding and engaging the world. The combination of these capacities makes us wholly intelligent. Dr. Howard Gardner, the first to premise multiple intelligences (MI) through his observations of children and adults, came to the hypothesis that people have a wide range of capacities.[7] As already stated, Gardner acknowledges many of us have probably experienced at some time in our lives a person considered intelligent but exhibiting the worst possible one-on-one interactions or lacking the ability for working within a team. This person may have been unable to communicate well, engage other people with civility, or was outright arrogant, demonstrating superiority over others who did not possess their intellectual acuity, i.e., the ability to expound facts, manipulate figures, or analyze and solve problems.

Gardner has identified a number of intelligences human beings seem to possess and exhibit. The capacities or intelligences that Gardner identified are Linguistic, Logical/Mathematical, Musical, Bodily-kinesthetic, Spatial, Naturalist, Existential, Interpersonal, and Intrapersonal (see Appendix 1 for definitions of these intelligences).

The most important intelligences for our work here are *Intrapersonal* and *Interpersonal*. These two intelligences are defined as follows[8]:

- Intrapersonal Intelligence *involves the capacity for understanding oneself, of having an **effective working model of oneself**. This includes understanding one's own desires, fears, and capacities and using such information effectively for regulating one's own life.*

- Interpersonal Intelligence *denotes a person's capacity for understanding intentions, motivations, and **desires of other people*** and, consequently, to work effectively with others.

Developing these two areas of MI, which may come through trial and error, can impact our relationships and overall sense of well-being, the central ingredients of EI. Mounting research confirms that individuals can improve their levels of EI (both intrapersonal and interpersonal) by recognizing personal areas of strength and weakness and then going through a process of emotional unlearning and relearning.[9]

Emotional learning involves reframing ineffective habits of thought, feeling, and action that are deeply ingrained in an individual. One cannot accomplish this type of learning in a one-day seminar, but it can be achieved gradually *if individuals are motivated to change. Discovering You* provides an opportunity for increasing your awareness and for setting goals based on this discovery. Your journey of transformation continues as you begin taking actions to improve the EI competencies that have a direct impact on your life and relationships and allow the Spirit to help you "put on the new self, created to be like God in true righteous and holiness" (Eph 4:24).

Personal Motivation for the EI Process

Most people only become motivated to change after experiencing a significant emotional event that some term a wake-up call. This wake-up call may come via a health crisis, a relationship meltdown, the loss of a career or job, financial stress or ruin, the death of someone dear, or some other emotionally painful event. Individuals are then faced with a choice of either learning something from the crisis and growing, or suppressing their inner conflict and digging deep into the safety of their own world.[10] This inner conflict may be summed up by the words of Dr. Morris Massey, author of *What You Are Is Where You Were When*: "It is a tragedy that people are dying eight hours every day." By this Massey means there are many working in careers or enmeshed in life situations that, like a slow death, kill them a little more morning after morning, day after day.[11]

Discovering You provides tools that may be utilized for voluntarily making changes in your life for the purpose of leading you to a fuller awareness of your EI. This process will take intentional effort, motivation, an emotional commitment, the support of others and openness to the Spirit. An honest self-reflection at the beginning creates a climate of hope and optimism. The question you must answer is, Am I willing to undertake this journey that leads to a lasting personal transformation? This query will determine your success in the effort.

The following exercise deals with your expectations related to your personal journey of discovery and change. The questions are designed to prompt reflection on your reason for wanting to develop a more resilient EI that can lead to becoming more effective intrapersonally and interpersonally.

The instructions are simple. Reflect on the following questions as honestly as possible. Take time to consider your answers candidly and *write out* whatever first comes to your mind. Responding to these questions mentally without writing down your answers tends to short-circuit this exercise. Personal reflection coupled with the act of writing provides the greatest opportunity for learning something new about yourself or reinforcing what you already understand.

Expectations

INTRAPERSONAL/SELF: *What is my goal for taking the needed time for personal self-reflection, assessment, and feedback from others as I work through this material?*

_____

_____

_____

_____

_____

_____

_____

_____

_____

_____

INTERPERSONAL/SOCIAL: *What is my hope for becoming more effective in how I relate to other people?*

_____

_____

_____

_____

_____

_____

_____

_____

_____

What Is Ahead?

In this section, we briefly examined the why behind EI, the benefits of becoming emotionally self-aware, and a reason why motivation is an essential tool for this life process.[12] In the next sections, you will begin identifying two spheres of life, your *Best-self* (step one) and your *Today-self* (step two). In both steps, you examine how you can work steadily toward living with a more refined EI and effective personal relationships. This diagram visually describes the activities you will work with in the remaining sections (*Best-self* is Step One; *Today-self* is Step Two; personal growth plan is Step Three.)

CONTINUOUS DISCOVERY

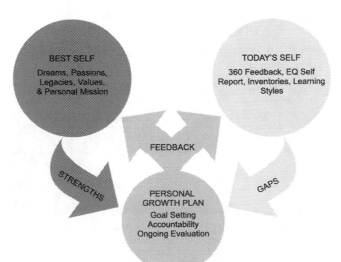

The diagram's title is "Continuous Discovery" because that is the bottom line of EI work. Learning the lessons about yourself is a lifelong process as you attempt to increase your strengths and close the gaps between your *Today-self* and *Best-self.* The work ahead starts with identifying your *Best-self,* that is, what you have always believed God intended you to be in life; it is the quiet whisper or tugging at your heart. This work will be followed by understanding your *Today-self,* that is, what you currently are, how you are currently living and reacting to and within your world.

The final step will be developing a *personal growth plan.* This plan must contain continuous adjustment of goals, being accountable for your progress, and constantly monitoring/evaluating your growth. All these elements are essential for closing the gaps you identify and increasing your level of EI.

Creating your personal mission statement and completing your *personal growth plan* will be the focus of the first step. It is through these two tools that you will identify and become aware of inaccurate self-perceptions while strengthening your EI.

STEP ONE

Listening to Your Best-self:
Who God Created You to Become

"Trust in the Lord with all your heart and lean not on your own understanding; in all your ways submit to him, and he will make your paths straight."
Proverbs 3:5-6

"Who in the world am I? Ah, that's the great puzzle."
Lewis Carroll (1832-1898)
English mathematician &
author of *Alice in Wonderland*

Personal growth and living effectively does not happen by chance. It is a series of choices we make starting with what we believe to be the life mission or calling set before us—our *Best-self.* This is in essence what we believe about whom we were created to be and the path we hope to walk during life. The discovery of your *Best-self* provides you the opportunity to be still and listen to your passions, dreams, desired legacies, and core values.

What follows is a sequentially structured step exercise designed to help you discover and write your personal mission. By honestly working through each step, you will be able to discover your own personal mission statement. Your mission will emerge and lead you to transformation as you work with this exercise *over time*. The exercise will also assist you in determining personal goals and action steps for developing your EI.

Work carefully through each of the four sequential steps listed in this exercise: Step 1—*Passion & Dreams*; Step 2—*Legacy*; Step 3—*Core Values*; and Step 4—*Personal Mission Statement.* The more careful and reflective you are throughout this process, the greater the likelihood you will discover what is deeply important for living a life that is "pleasing to God" and builds up his kingdom (Rom 12:1-2; Heb 13:21). Ultimately, you will discover a sense of purpose that like a beacon will draw you toward giving your best efforts to others and to God.

In our positions at Anderson University, we are often in conversation with students who are seeking to discover their direction in life and what God is calling them to undertake. With a lack of self-awareness in selecting their major area of study, many feel trapped and struggle to stay motivated as they move deeper into a subject area. As previously noted, our current jobs provide us many opportunities to fulfill our separate but related personal mission statements. We have personally used the step process that we outline over the coming pages to write our own mission statements. It now helps us guide students toward their passions, goals, personal mission, and ultimately the *Best-self* God intends for them. This process helps them no longer remain trapped or struggle with what their futures will hold. We offer this step process to you as well with the hope it will lead you to places of discovery and fulfillment.

Step 1: Identifying Your Passion and Dreams

Perhaps as a child you were asked, "What do you want to be when you grow up?" This question, which brought answers like "fireman," "mommy," "teacher," "policeman," or "the president" from an 8-year-old, is just as critically important for you to consider at this juncture in your life. Taking time to reflect on this question may spark passion or dreams long forgotten. Discovering your passion and dreams provides the motivation to change and may inspire others to follow your example.

Somewhere along the way, others may have told you that your dreams were not what you should pursue or be when you grew up. Over your formative years, parents, grandparents, teachers, or others of influence may have started pointing you toward careers where there was more money compared to your dream job, abounding prestige awaiting its fulfillment, or occupations where you would be the third generation to carry it on. In the book *Primal Leadership*, the authors call this concept the *"ought-self"* and caution the reader not to become trapped in its box.[1]

An awareness that leads to healthy EI, and ultimately effective relationships, requires a person to step back and take a moment to listen to their own passion and what God might be offering to them. A way for stepping back and reflecting on what you believe about life can be accomplished through developing a personal mission statement (as you will do later). The process of creating a personal mission statement can move you toward grasping the ideal image of who you believe you were created to be.

Parker Palmer, in his book *Let Your Life Speak;* writes,

> Before you tell your life what you intend to do with it, listen for what it intends to do with you. Before you tell your life what truths and values you have decided to live up to, let your life tell you what truths you embody, what values you represent.[2]

Palmer offers encouragement to the reader for investing time in personal reflection for discovering what you were created to become—your *Best-self.* So, at this point in life, consider answering the question, What do you want to be when you grow up? As Po Bronson writes in *What Should I Do With My Life*,

> We all have passions if we choose to see them. Most of us don't get epiphanies. We don't get clarity. Our purpose doesn't arrive neatly packaged as destiny. We only get a whisper. A blank, nonspecific urge. That's how it starts.[3]

The process of personal change begins when you know the difference between what people believe you *ought* to do and what you perceive to be your *Best-self,* what you hear your life and God saying to you. As you progress in your personal discovery, honest reflection is an essential teacher. Patient reflection provides the insights needed for uncovering the path from where you are currently to where you hope to be in the future. Scazzero again reminds us, "Relax. Change is slow. It's a whole life change, a whole life journey."[4]

If you are not living as you want, you must ask the question, Why? Honest and penetrating seeking educates you about what matters in your life and what keeps you from truly living purposefully. Self-examination begins the progress toward discovering an identity that reflects your God-given passions and desires.

The questions on the following pages are meant to help you consider what you believe to be your *Best-self*—the person you were created to be. Take time to *write out* your responses to these questions. Be honest with yourself in each of the statements. If you do not have an immediate answer, allow the question to germinate in your thinking for a while before you answer. Dream big!

Questions for Identifying Passions and Dreams

Describe a typical day if you were living your ideal life with no barriers (time, money, etc.). What would you be doing to bring personal fulfillment and live pleasing to God?

_____
_____
_____
_____
_____
_____

Where would you ideally enjoy living? What is it about this place that would be fulfilling?

_____
_____
_____
_____
_____
_____
_____

Whom would you have around you regularly who would bring you fulfillment? What are the characteristics of these individuals that are important to you?

_____

_____

_____

_____

_____

Whom would you want to trade jobs with and why?

_____

_____

_____

_____

_____

_____

_____

Whom do you respect the most and why?

_____

_____

_____

_____

_____

_____

The questions from the preceding section are a means of introducing you to the work of discovering you. The insights you uncovered by answering the questions set the stage for transformation to your *Best-self*. The previous exercise also helps create parameters you may use to consider your own definition of success, which may be the opposite of what the world or others want from you.

Record a summary of your passions and dreams on your Self-Awareness Profile sheet in the appendix. The insights you record will be useful as you move to the next steps, where you will expand your answers and use them as you begin drafting a personal mission statement.

Step 2: Considering Your Legacy

Consider your life from the end. It is easy to judge what you want in life from this present moment, but it is quite another to have that desire fulfilled at the end of your life. Sometimes distractions and situations occur throughout your life that may move you to places you ultimately never intended to be or allowed you to stray from the path you believed was right and true.

In this step, it is important that you ponder and consider what you hope life will look like from the end of it. How do you want to be remembered and celebrated by your family, friends, and local or faith communities? Randy Travis, in his song "Three Wooden Crosses," reminds us, "It's not what you take when you leave this world behind you; it's what you leave behind you when you go."[5]

Perusing the obituaries of your local newspaper provides a spectrum of legacies people created during their living years, whether intentionally or by chance. The following caught our eye when we looked at some obituaries in our local newspaper to see the range of how people spent their days: "She lived to help others." "He was a flea market fan." "She was a loving, caring mother and grandmother to her children and grandchildren." By reflecting on how your final day might be described, you can begin making choices as to where you will spend your time, talent, and treasures during the present to fulfill the plans God has for your life.

Complete the following questions as the next step toward writing your personal mission statement. Review your answers to questions already considered in the previous step while working through this section. Doing so will add additional insight as you focus on these questions.

Questions for Identifying My Legacy

If you discovered today that you had just six months to live, what would you focus on? What three items of importance would you want to achieve before your life's end?

_____

_____

_____

_____

_____

_____

What do you want said about you by your family, friends, and local or faith communities at the end of your life…in your obituary?

_____

_____

_____

_____

_____

At an old age, when you think back across your life, what will make you feel that your life has been worthwhile and bring a smile of satisfaction to your face? What type of life will receive the words "well done, good and faithful servant" (Luke 9:17)?

_____

_____

_____

_____

_____

What do you believe God is asking you to undertake or be during your lifetime? What keeps you from acknowledging and accepting this belief?

_____

_____

_____

_____

_____

What makes your heart pound when you consider doing this thing or when you realize you may not be able to accomplish this dream or goal?

_____

_____

_____

_____

As you review your responses to the previous questions, **write out three to five legacies** that will accurately represent what you desire to leave behind (what might be written in the newspaper for your obituary). An example might read, "I want to be remembered for being a loving spouse and parent, a supportive friend, an active community volunteer, and an accomplished skydiver."

In the space below, write out these legacies:

_____

_____

_____

_____

_____

_____

Spend time pondering these life legacies (from your writing above) that you desire to leave as your service to this world. Answer this question, What do these legacies have in common? What is (are) the theme(s) that connect these legacies together?

Using our previous example, you might notice themes such as, "I desire to be a *loving person* (related to spouse, children, friends); an *encouraging person* (related to spouse, children, friends; *encouraging* is a synonym of the concept of being supportive); a *committed person* (related to spouse, children, friends, community)." These characteristics—loving person, encouraging person, and committed person—are much larger and encompassing in scope than roles like parent, friend, volunteer, or skydiver.

It is important to keep track in writing of these themes as you discover or undercover them. Take time now to record your legacy themes on your Self-Awareness Profile located in the appendix.

Step 3: Deciding Your Core Values

This step will help you identify your core values through making forced choices. Many individuals are in careers that conflict with the areas that are very important in their lives. Becky experienced these feelings of dissonance, as her position in corporate finance required her to spend long hours of detailed analytical work, relocate, and travel frequently. The opportunity to complete a Myers-Briggs personality assessment in a corporate training program proved to be a life-changing event for Becky. Her personality type was an ENFP: "The careers chosen most often by ENFPs (according to our research with people already in work) include psychology, entrepreneurship, marketing, training, human resources, management, academia."[6]

Learning what it meant to be an ENFP, Becky began to reflect on why she had originally double-majored in teaching and accounting in college. That assessment brought clarity to why she felt dissonance. An individual with personality preferences of ENFP is the exact opposite of the ISTJ type, who naturally enjoys analytical accounting/finance type work. After taking time for personal reflection, assessment, and prayer, Becky began realizing that pursing her lifelong dream to teach business classes at the university level would be more in line with her core values and strengths. This career change required obtaining her doctorate. As a result, teaching has been a source of personal and spiritual fulfillment in Becky's life.

One of Stephen Covey's insights applies here and jabs enough that it might be useful for nudging us awake. It is about pain. In his book *First Things First*, Covey observes, "Much of our pain in life comes from the sense that we're succeeding in one role (of life) at the expense of others, possibly even more important roles."[7] Dr. Phil McGraw, today's in-your-face analyst, is a little blunter when he lasers in, forcefully inquiring, "Is it working for you?" If we have enough pain and dissonance from our current situations and life journey thus far, acknowledging that pain and finding *healthy* remedies for it might really reshape us.

Core Values Exercise

Quickly review the following columns of words below so that you are familiar with them.[8]

peace	wealth	integrity
joy	happiness	love
success	recognition	friendship
family	fame	truth
authenticity	wisdom	power
status	influence	justice
nobility	fairness	virtuous
gentleness	kindness	goodness
purity	hope	honesty
freedom	faith	honor
dignity	respect	equality
charity	simplicity	other? _____

Follow these steps below as you refer back to this list of core values:

1. After reviewing these columns of words, consider the following questions: Which values from the columns, if absent from my life, will diminish me as a human being or what I believe about myself? Which values, if not in my life, will keep me from being who I really believe I am in relationship to God and others?" **Circle ten core values that you think accurately answer these questions.**

2. From the ten values you have circled, **cross off the five** that are least critical to you as you reflect on the questions from question 1.

3. Now, with those five core values chosen, answer this question: For what **three** values am I willing to suffer persecution or gladly die? These three core values are important ingredients for writing and living your mission statement. Now record your three core values on your Self-Awareness Profile worksheet.

Step 4: Writing Your Personal Mission Statement

At this point, try drafting a personal mission statement. From the first three steps completed in this section, consider your passion/dreams, the legacies you hope to leave after your death, and your chosen core life values (the three identified from the exercise in Step 3). Take time to think carefully about each of the previous exercises. Look closely at your answers and determine if there is any overlap in your responses. For example, you might ask yourself:

- Are there any answers that were similar in each exercise? If so, what are they?
- If I look carefully and thoughtfully, are the core values I chose reflected in my dreams or legacies? If so, what are they?
- If someone asked me to give them a summary of these three exercises and what I learned, what would I tell them?
- How would I describe what I feel from completing these three exercises in no more than two sentences?

Try taking the ideas that are possibly wandering rag-tag through your mind and putting them into a sentence. (The last question above may be a starting point.) Remember that it does not have to be a polished sentence or statement during this first attempt at writing your personal mission. *Personal mission writing is not an exact science but a fleshing out of your thoughts, dreams, and beliefs.*

Continually rewriting, pondering, rewriting, and pondering your personal mission using these guidelines will eventually make the statement you are writing now more crisp, concise, and clear *over time.* An observation by David might illustrate this point best related to working on your mission over time and allowing it to unfold and become more precise. He observed, "Some time ago while watching butterflies, I noticed they do not fly in a straight line, that is, from point A to point B. Now that does not mean they do not have a target; it just means they fly in apparently random patterns to get to their destination. It may feel in mission-writing work that you are flying randomly through a disconnected series of words and thoughts. However, it will get you from point A to point B. You must keep your eye on the target."

Your personal mission statement should not be cast in concrete, never to be revisited or clarified. It should be reviewed, revised, and updated over time. While the core idea/ theme should not change, the words should become clearer as you mull over the concepts and phrases. Take time regularly for reviewing and thinking over your mission. Make those changes as you feel appropriate and more defining of your mission statement.[9]

MY PERSONAL MISSION STATEMENT

_____

_____

_____

_____

_____

_____

After you write your initial personal mission statement, test it by asking, Can I really affect my world and the people in it by living out my mission? If yes, then how? If not, you might revise your mission statement in order to keep you actively working toward its fulfillment.

This personal mission statement will help guide you and give you focus. The mission should be challenging *to you* and something for which *you are* passionate. It does not have to be a statement that is exciting to others, but it must pull from you the best of your abilities, passions, and actions. When you read your mission statement, it should give you motivation for fulfilling it or even make your blood pressure rise because you long to complete this part of your life.

Laurie Beth Jones, national bestselling author of *Jesus, CEO, The Path*, and *Jesus in Blue Jeans*, gives a few simple guidelines for writing your personal mission statement that might help at this juncture.[10]

1. Your mission statement should be a single sentence.
2. A 12-year-old should understand your mission statement and be able to recite it.
3. You should be able to repeat your mission from memory…at "gun point"…as if your life depended on it.

A note is in order about your mission statement being a single sentence. A concise sentence in English is normally between 8 and 12 words (like this sentence). If your initial mission statement is longer than 8 to 12 words, try rewriting it. The more concise the statement, the easier it is for a 12-year-old to understand and for you to recite.

You may also find that spending time in a personal annual retreat will help you get clearer about your purpose and mission for your work and life. You might take a one-day retreat each year to a place of solitude with the purpose of reviewing your mission and setting goals related to it. We recommend a place devoid of distractions so that you might prayerfully reflect on your mission and wisely construct goals that will accomplish your dreams.[11] Remember, Jesus regularly retreated to a solitary place to pray and find refreshment (Matt 14:13; Mark 1:35; Luke 4:42).

Now here is the real point of this mission-writing exercise. The ultimate purpose for creating a personal mission statement is not just to have a statement. It is necessary for engaging your life—how you want to intentionally live it, what choices you will make, what goals you will set, and what effect you will have had on your world once you leave this planet. We are convinced that if you construct a personal mission statement and *live it daily*, you will influence not just your immediate world but generations yet to come.

Personal transformation begins with increased self-awareness and discovery. This step serves as the solid foundation for your further discovery. It serves as a portrait of your *Best-self.* The responses you gave to the exercises in this section will be essential as you progress toward creating a personal growth plan, which if implemented will help you move closer to what you hope to become during your life. Take a few moments to record your personal mission statement on your Self-Awareness Profile in the appendix.

STEP TWO

Discovering Your Today-self:
Your Strengths and Gaps or Growth Areas

"I have no idea how I would have learned the truth about myself and my calling without the mistakes I have made..."
Parker Palmer
Let Your Life Speak

"There is only one corner of the universe you can be certain of improving, and that's your own self."
Aldous Huxley (1894-1963)
Time Must Have a Stop

Up to this point, you have been focused on self-reflection to gain a better understanding of your *Best-self*—the person you would like and were created to be. By thoughtful completion of the exercises in the previous step, you have started down the path of increased personal awareness—the foundation for building EI. This second step will guide you further on your journey of awareness by discovering your *Today-self* through some assessments and feedback from others.

Asking others for feedback will assist you in your transition from what you are today to what you want to become. This is a humbling experience, but it is critical for the development process. One of the signs of a strengthening EI is the ability to ask and receive critique from others. Additionally, you will develop a more accurate picture of your *Today-self* when you invite others, such as a mentor, coach, or a person deeply trusted, to assist you in this ongoing life change.

Tools for Strengthening your EI

360-Degree Inventory and Feedback

In Step One, you worked privately in designing the vision of your *Best-self* or who you intend to be at the end of this process. In this Step Two, you will check what you privately perceive against reality—that which others see and experience when they interact with you. Knowing what exists in the gap is essential for moving toward a more developed EI and for focusing on your strengths while identifying opportunities for growth.

In order to get the most from this tool, we trust you are open to hearing what others disclose to you. You might consider rereading your answers to the questions in Step One of this book where you were asked to reflect on your expectations related to developing your EI. This may reassure you while giving you courage for taking this vitally important step toward greater personal awareness.

We also remind you not to focus solely on what may be perceived as your personal weaknesses. Rather, we hope you will focus on your strengths while discovering how you might "bring along" or improve your weaknesses. Peter Drucker, the father of management theory, often stressed that we should be focusing on our strengths while improving our perceived weaknesses over time. If viewed properly, this can be a wonderful time of exploration and insight rather than one of inner turmoil or fear.

The theme of this tool centers on inviting people into the discovery process for identifying both your strengths and weaknesses. While this 360-Degree Tool is valuable, we want to employ a cautionary note from the outset: *We encourage you in this feedback section to choose people who know you well, but not just from your workplace or those who might fit the category of acquaintance rather than friends or those you trust.* If you are to receive the most accurate feedback regarding both your strengths and weaknesses, we encourage you to find people in the categories we describe. *These people, again, must know you well, not just as an acquaintance or someone with whom you have only a rare encounter.* These people should also be ones you consider safe and personally interested in your future and well-being.

Daniel Goleman provides two important criteria for those you choose: "1) the people who participate in this feedback actually interact with you on a regular basis, and; 2) you reveal yourself to them, that is, you have been in an open, honest relationship with them."[1] In other words, you should provide this exercise to those who really know you and do not simply know about you.

Step One—Identifying Your Partners

The following box gives you categories of people for this exercise. Next to the category, place a person's name that meets the criteria outlined in the previous two paragraphs and the suggestions of Daniel Goleman. Make sure you have at least five people of the seven categories identified. As authors, we often have people say they could only identify two or three people. This is unfortunate, because it will not provide you with an accurate feedback portrait and it may allow you to identify those responding to you. This identification may cause you frustration, emotional pain, or strain your relationships as you attempt to understand why the person would have responded this way about you. So we encourage you to have at least five individuals in this assessment process.

Categories of People to Contact for this Feedback Exercise	The Person's Name
A co-worker in your department	
A subordinate or someone you lead	
A peer at your workplace who may not work in your department	
A person from your church	
A person from a civic organization	
A family member with whom you regularly interact	
Your closest friend	

Step Two—Inviting Help

Once you have chosen these people, it is important to ask them to join you in the process of your personal transformation. You should explain very clearly why you are undertaking this venture and why you are seeking their help. Explain that their role is to give you honest, candid feedback about both your weaknesses *and* your strengths.

Step Three—Providing the 360-Degree Feedback Inventory

Copy the 360° Feedback form found in the appendix. Give these feedback pages to the people you have identified for assisting you in this venture. Permit them just a day or two for completing the sheets and then return them to you. You should provide a plain envelope that you hand address or otherwise make anonymous for the return of the feedback sheet. You should instruct these individuals to give you this information without placing their name or identity on it.

Step Four—Reflecting on the Responses

After you have collected and read all the responses, you may want to ask a trusted friend, a coach, or mentor to help you reflect on sections or comments you do not understand. Ask these individuals to help you assess the collective insights gained as a way of growing, changing in positive ways, and for developing your EI. You may consider some of the information you received as negative or as deficiencies. However, remember that this conversation should be full of hope and optimism, not dejection and self-abasement. Your attitude and desire for learning from this exercise will be important when receiving the results from this process.

Step Five—What Do the Responses Uncover?

After you receive this written feedback and seek additional clarification, consider what these responses tell you. Look for the patterns emerging from these various people and then compare these patterns with the *Best-self* you identified in Step One. For example, a number of individuals may note you appear not to listen when you are with them. The gaps you discover provide the opportunity for emotional and relational improvement as you work on goal setting in Step Three.

360-Degree Feedback from others

My strengths as perceived by others

_____

_____

_____

_____

_____

Identified areas for improvement

_____

_____

_____

_____

_____

Record a summary of your 360° feedback on your Self-Awareness Profile in the appendix, noting particularly the areas you want to improve in your relationships.

Considering Hidden Areas in Our Lives

We all have areas in our lives that we hide from others. We know things about ourselves we are careful not to reveal. Yet it is important in our work of assessment to examine these hidden areas. The concept we are inviting you to explore in this section rests on insights by Parker Palmer, author, founder, and senior partner of the Center for Courage and Renewal. These hidden areas are often those we want to avoid or do not want to acknowledge about ourselves. These desires or intentions can cause our downfall if we do not attend to them. You can explore what we are describing through answering the question implied by Palmer: "What behavior or practice would cause my downfall, personal destruction, or wound those closest to me if I gave into its allure or acted on it?"

This hidden area might be a desire or passion that if indulged could ruin your life. As Palmer writes in *Let Your Life Speak: Listening for the Voice of Vocation*,

> My life is not only about my strengths and virtues; it is also about my liabilities and my limits, my trespasses and my shadows. An inevitable

though often ignored dimension of the quest of 'wholeness' is that we must embrace what we dislike or find shameful about ourselves as well as what we are confident and proud of.[2]

Palmer suggests we surface these hidden areas and acknowledge they are a part of our private lives. Once acknowledged, we can be on the lookout for the tempting moments. Peter Scazzero supports Palmer by noting we must face our shadows. Scazzero says shadows are not always a sinful place related to morality or ethics, but they can be an attitude where we are "critical and unloving; feel superior to others or believe we know more than others. It may also be wanting to be liked, so we avoid conflict or speaking truthfully in situations. As we acknowledge these shadow places we join God in taking off the old and putting on the new (Eph 4:22)."[3]

A helpful tool is to share these shadow areas with someone who will keep you accountable and always moving toward a stronger EI. This practice, while hard, may be very freeing. It may be that you will find a counselor, coach, or clergy more useful in this method of developing a stronger EI than an accountability partner as described in the appendix. The authors (Becky and David) have both utilized accountability partners for many years, Christian friends who keep them accountable for their faith, family, and relationships.

As stated at the beginning, self-knowledge that comes by asking others to participate is a personal risk. Yet, it may be the most significant part of your change. Without the assistance of other people, we have the tendency to feed on our own thoughts and ideals, which may be incorrect assumptions or projections. We may also justify all we do without the balance of outside perspectives.[4]

If the people you have chosen have been honest and forthright with you in the 360-Degree Feedback, take their suggestions for strengthening the relationships you have with them. The residual or ripple effect will be that most other relationships you have in life will benefit from the strengthening of those relationships closest to you.

Other Useful Instruments

To this point, you have been guided through personal reflection activities (for uncovering your *Best-self*) and feedback from others (for starting the process of identifying your *Today-self*). These two areas of awareness are useful and important mechanisms for shaping your life, developing effective EI, and making lasting personal change. While the methods used to this point are important, there are, however, other inventories available for helping you discover the possible gaps.

What follows is an overview of the assessment tools we recommend for gaining additional insight. We are aware of many other available assessments; however, we have selected the following tools based on our personal experience and use of them over the past several years.

Many assessment inventories are copyrighted or best completed in conjunction with working through a trained consultant, thus they are not contained in this chapter. We encourage you to locate these inventories through the means we describe or to find a trainer who can be of assistance in using these tools. You might also consider working with a local college or university. Many educational institutions have career counseling centers that utilize these instruments.

Some of these inventories may also be located through the Internet. Internet tools may be free of charge or a fee might be associated with them. Remember to seek out the most reputable sites when taking instruments via the Internet. Nevertheless, whether you seek out these tools through educational institutions, career counselors, or via the Internet, they are one of the best ways for determining other facets of your *Today-self*.

Record a summary of your findings on your Self-Awareness Profile if you choose to complete these suggested assessments. We recommend using some or all of these tools for rounding out your personal discovery process. Remember to use them in conjunction with what you have learned in the prior exercise concerning how you are actually perceived by others. The assessments are by nature self-reporting and may not actually reflect what others experience each time they interact with you. So use these tools not as an end result but as a means for your ongoing work of personal change.

Emotional Intelligence (EQ) Assessment

During the last decade, the concept of EI has been recognized as an area of growing importance for experiencing well-being and establishing effective relationships. This increased interest has resulted in the emergence of numerous books, assessment tools, and training programs focused on the measurement and development of EI. Research studies continue confirming that EI is more important than IQ in predicting the success of leaders, students, financial advisors, and others.

If you are interested in reviewing information related to leading EQ studies, assessments, and training programs, you are encouraged to access websites and books by authors such as Daniel Goleman, Reuven Bar-On, Richard Boyatzis, Steven Stein, and Peter Scazzero. Many EQ assessments are now available online as a self-report or multi-rater, or may be purchased by contacting Rebecca Haskett at bahaskett@ anderson.edu. Dr. Haskett is certified to administer the Bar-On EQ-i and Talent Smarts EIA assessments.

EQ Self-Report

My strengths are:

_____

_____

_____

_____

Gaps or areas for improvement:

_____

_____

_____

_____

The Value of Other Assessments

There are many assessments that are useful in understanding your strengths and areas for growth. These assessments are valuable tools for helping you identify how you interact with others, whether one on one or in a group setting.

We recommend the following assessments or inventories. You may find them on the Internet (often free) or at some charge by the purveyor. For the best results, we encourage you to take these inventories offered by someone trained to help interpret the information. There may be easy methods to get results, but utilizing them without someone trained to help may provide an inaccurate assessment of who you are and how you engage others.

- *Myers-Briggs Type Indicator* (This inventory focuses on understanding preferences, individual differences, and how one relates these characteristics to people or situations.)
- *The DiSC Inventory* (This inventory is similar to the Myers-Briggs Type Indicator.)

- *Enneagram Inventory* (This inventory is similar to DiSC and Myers-Briggs Type Indicator. Its development comes out of the long history of spiritual formation.)
- *Learning Styles* (This inventory identifies how we prefer to take in and utilize information/data, whether for learning or problem solving.)
- *Firo B* (This inventory focuses on how we interact during group, work settings, or mediate between conflicting ideas or situations within a group.)
- *Spiritual Gifts* ("A spiritual gift is an expression of the Holy Spirit in the life of believers which empowers them to serve the body of Christ, the church.")[5]
- *StrengthsFinder* (This inventory helps people discover their unique combination of strengths.)

Personal assessment tools used in conjunction with the previous exercises will give you a clearer understanding of your strengths as well as those places you will note are gaps between your *Best-self* and *Today-self.* All of these exercises, however, are of little use unless you take the cumulative results you have recorded on your Self-Awareness Profile and begin setting a course of action.

In Step Three, you will be guided in developing your Personal Growth Plan for strengthening your EI. By setting goals based on your personal reflection (Step One— *Best-self*) and assessments (Step Two—*Today-self*), you will be choosing to take steps toward fulfilling your personal mission and what God has both created and invited you to become.

STEP THREE

Intentionally Moving Ahead: Developing Your Personal Growth Plan

"You are what you repeatedly do. Excellence is not a singular act but a habit."
Aristotle (384-322 BC)

"I never did anything worth doing by accident; nor did any of
my inventions come by accident; they came by work."
Thomas Alva Edison (1847-1931)

"Commit your work to the Lord, and then your plans will succeed."
Proverbs 16:3 NLT

Whenever people try to change habits of how they think and act, they must reverse decades of learning that resides in heavily traveled, highly reinforced neural circuitry, built up over years of repeating that habit. That's why making lasting change requires a strong commitment to a future vision of oneself—especially during stressful times or amid growing responsibilities.[1]

You have completed a significant amount of work over these pages. The work focused you on your *Best-self* and *Today-self.* You are now ready to utilize your work for completing the important task of goal setting. What action steps will it take to make lasting personal changes and develop effective EI? Priorities and goal setting are essential to any movement.

Step Three will lead you through developing goals based on your Self-Awareness Profile. You will also be offered some tools that you may choose to use that will afford greater success in completing your goals. It is our hope that you will give considerable attention to and work in this section, as much as you may have in all the previous material. Without setting and working on goals synthesized from your Self-Awareness Profile, you may not reach your intended plan of developing a stronger EI.[2]

Goal-Setting for Growth

Each of the following steps leads naturally to the next so that you will achieve goal attainment via goal setting and action planning.

Step 1: Reviewing Your Self-Awareness Profile

Establishing priorities and setting goals must be related to your mission and vision of your *Best-self* as compared to your current state—*Today-self.* Your personal mission statement is the foundation of all goal setting. Plans or goals made without your personal mission at the center may take you to fun places but not the ones that bring your mission into reality.

A review of your completed Self-Awareness Profile is the initial step in gaining the insight needed for beginning the goal setting process of your Personal Growth Plan. Consider your unique strengths, talents, passion, and gifts that you would like to further develop and utilize. It is also important to consider the gaps or areas of growth where your current reality is hindering your progress.

Looking at your Self-Awareness Profile summary sheet, summarize your thoughts as you begin to consider potential goals.

What are personal strengths I possess that I must continue developing to make them even stronger?

_____

_____

_____

_____

_____

_____

What are some gaps or areas for growth that may exist between my Best-self and Today-self?

_____

_____

_____

_____

_____

_____

Step 2: Successful Goal Attainment in Step 1 by Managing Your Time, Fears, and Stressors

Your potential for personal growth, fulfillment, and closing the gaps are closely tied to the daily choices you make concerning how you spend your time. The strengths you want to increase and the gaps you want to narrow can only happen if you focus your use of time.

Simply put, using time is a daily choice of how to expend 86,400 seconds, 1,440 minutes, or 24 hours. These choices stem from our attitudes about time, ability to focus, and willingness to set goals that take us to our desired destinations. If you make conscious choices of how you use your time, we know from experience you will succeed in creating an effective life and reaching your desire of increasing your EI. Changing your attitude and recapturing unfocused use of time is not complicated, but it does take a commitment to balancing life demands.

You may limit your chance for successful transformation if self-talk relates to fears and stressors that may cause you to lose focus. Setting goals and using time effectively are essential for growth and change, but fear and stressors may keep you from ever implementing your plans.

We offer you some exercises in the appendix to assist you in identifying areas you may need to address, such as Time Management—Determining Priorities (Appendix 3), Personal Time Bandits (Appendix 4), Identifying and Overcoming Your Fears (Appendix 5), and Stressors—"Gnawing Sense of Anxiety" (GSA) (Appendix 6). If you do not confront these items head-on, you may never reach the level of change that leads to a new way of living.

STOP RIGHT NOW IN THIS STEP. Go to the appendices mentioned above. Complete all these activities. After you have completed these activities, complete the following:

What are the three most important insights I gained about myself and my use of time by completing these exercises? (Be specific).

_____

_____

_____

_____

_____

_____

What three things will I confront about myself and commit to changing related to how I use my time that will move me closer to my goals? (Be very specific and place a date as to when you will begin this change.)

_____

_____

_____

_____

_____

_____

Step 3: Using your Mission, Strengths, Areas of Growth, and Commitment for Wise Time Usage and Setting Goals (i.e., living out your Personal Growth Plan)

After completing Steps 1 and 2, you are now ready to move forward with creating and then living out your Personal Growth Plan. In this step, you will be more specific in thoughtfully developing goals and detailed action steps. Setting personal goals will help you decide where to focus your time and energy. Goal setting can be overwhelming at times. Initially we advocate setting only three or four goals for the next year—along with action steps necessary to achieve each goal—with target dates.

Most people do not have written goals based on their mission statements or areas of growth. Not writing down goals makes those that you may have rattling around in your mind a simple wish list. *Goals are real and achievable only when they are on paper.* If your goals do not have incremental steps, it is too easy to put off starting on your goals because they might be vague in your mind. It is also helpful to establish a timeframe for addressing each step. Periodically checking off action steps when completed provides encouragement and motivation for continued work. If possible, do something daily related to achieving your goals.

When setting your goals, it is useful to consider your whole person—physical, emotional, mental, and spiritual. It is useful to develop goals in all areas of your life. The following is merely an example of how to write goals based on your mission. Once you understand this process, utilize the form on the back of your Self-Awareness Profile for recording your own goals and tracking your progress.

An Example

(A Personal Growth Plan based on mission, strengths, and growth areas)

Personal mission: Instilling the love of learning through teaching excellence.

Strengths: I love reading extensively.

Gaps or growth areas: I need more skill in classroom management for student behavior.

GOAL: Develop a comprehensive reading plan *(for increasing strengths)*	Target Date	Completed
ACTION STEPS OR TASKS: 1. Determine what books I want to read during the next year. 2. Begin reading one book each month. 3. Write what I learned in the front of the books I own or incorporate the ideas into my classroom teaching.	By Nov. By Jan. By March	X

GOAL: Learn the skills needed for classroom management *(for closing the gaps that may cause students not to love learning; the focus of the mission)*	Target Date	Completed
ACTION STEPS OR TASKS: 1. Ask a co-worker teacher to observe my classroom management skills.	By Oct.	X
2. Ask a co-worker teacher for candid evaluation of my relational skills with students.	By Jan.	
3. Locate and enroll in a course on classroom management.	By March	

In the example above, you will notice that the mission serves as the anchor for the goals. If you want to "instill the love of learning through teaching excellence," then working on strengths and gaps via goals increases the likelihood that this mission will be realized over time. The goals coming out of the mission may be technical in nature, such as reading, but they should also incorporate relational strengths and gaps so that in time your EI improves.

Consider a final note related to the classroom management gap (between the ideal/mission and the reality): The co-worker teacher (see task 2) may candidly share that there are strengths ("You are a good listener") while sharing that you need to control impulses ("You regularly appear impatient or speak harshly to students"). Setting relational goals for improvement in both areas again will help this fictitious teacher become more emotionally successful in the future with the outcome that students may love learning as a result.[3]

Setting the Bar Higher for Personal Growth and Emotional Intelligence

Goal setting based on individual determination and commitment is possible. Many people succeed in the world through their own strength and motivation. In this section, however, we invite you to raise the bar a little higher by inviting others to keep you accountable for succeeding at your dreams and goals. We encourage you to set a higher standard of excellence by utilizing an accountability partner or board of directors. While not everyone will utilize this section, it is our experience that these two tools can increase one's growth and mission attainment.

Forming Your Accountability Partner Relationship

We mistakenly believe goal attainment and personal development are achieved through individual effort. Goal attainment and fully living our life legacies mean knowing two things. One is knowing our partners in the process. The second is understanding what resources are necessary for life's journey. We often forget partners because we believe goal attainment is about single handedly conquering life. However, if you peel back any tremendous success in the world, you will notice that other people (often thousands) were involved in the goal process just below the visible layer of reward for any one particular individual.

Personal growth is not an exact science. It is a relational development: internally, externally with others, as well as otherworldly with our Creator. While sometimes confusing, intense, and draining, this relational development will lead to a more successful life as well as relationships that are more effective.

We invite you to consider whom you will ask to help you become what you were intended to be (via use of an accountability partner, mentor, coach, or others). These partners could potentially be those that you selected in the section related to your 360° Feedback.

If you choose to set the bar higher by working with an accountability partner, there are some important criteria to consider when selecting individuals to assist you:

1. *Shared values*—This person has character values in common with you, such as integrity, concern for others, faith, etc.
2. *Outstanding listener*—This person, for the most part, is an effective communicator and does not dominate the conversation or spew out unending monologues of wisdom on how you live our life or deal with areas of concern or problems.
3. *Credibility/trustworthiness*—This person holds the confidence of others and can be trusted, period.
4. *Ability and willingness to provide honest feedback*—This individual honestly wants to help you grow and mature in your EI and faith.
5. *Easy to establish rapport and comfortable with the relationship of serving as an accountability partner.*

If you are interested in setting the bar for personal growth a little higher, then read Appendix 7 related to accountability partners. Implementing this relationship may feel a bit unnerving and is not for everyone, but it can prove to be the best tool for sustained emotional and relational growth.

Forming a Personal Board of Directors

Many individuals have people they want as mentors. We might seek their counsel or expertise in getting our jobs done or in understanding something new about ourselves. Maybe these mentors serve by helping us sort out the personal issues in our lives, such as our dreams, careers, plans, or avocations. In whatever capacity they serve, mentors will be essential to your self-knowledge, establishing personal mission, and spiritual direction. They can be very helpful in translating this personal awareness into daily activities.

This tool for raising the bar on your work toward effective EI is called Personal Board of Directors. To begin this activity, draw a board table on a separate sheet of paper like the diagram given in this section. In the seats around the board table you have drawn, place the names of the people you want to be on your Personal Board of Directors (see Appendix 7 for descriptions of accountability partners, coaches, and mentors for more information). Some of these individuals may already be active in your life, but other names represent people you want to have as support. As you complete this exercise, consider the questions listed in the center of the table as your guide for selecting people and for sharing this process with them.

TRUSTED FRIEND   SOMEONE YOU ADMIRE   SIMILAR SPIRITUAL GIFT

- Who is on your board of directors?
- What is their role on your board?
- Do these people know they are on your board? How?
- Have you told them or asked them to play a part in your life and development?
- Are these people going to be on your board forever or will they change at some point in time?
- What do you want from these people? Advice? Networking? Critique? Wisdom? Prayer? Other support?

ACCOUNTABILITY PARTNER   MENTOR   PERSONAL COACH

Once you have completed this exercise, it is time for action. You may find that having only one or two of the above noted partnerships will suffice at this point in your journey.

Begin by taking time to explain this process to the people you have selected. Answer any questions that they may have regarding what you expect from them or what commitments they are willing to make to this growth process.

Next, tell the people at the table that you value them and need their expertise for guiding you in this process of personal growth. They may already be your friends and mentors, but it is important to acknowledge them by sharing appreciation for their connection in your life. However, there may be names of people around that table who are not currently working with you. It is important to ask them if they are willing to accept this challenge of helping you realize your mission, goals, and dreams. You might ask them through a telephone call, letter, or over lunch. Nevertheless, the critical aspect is the asking.

Once you have answered any questions and confirmed these relationships, you should determine a regular time for meeting with them. In these meetings, you will share your written goals and progress. This group can also assist you in evaluating ideas or projects you are working on at present. As we hope you understand, the value and resource of this personal board are almost limitless.

It is our belief that we cannot grow without allowing others to challenge us—to take a risk that others can help shape and mold us into the person we want to become. Quite simply, the voices of other people keep us honest and challenge us to hear what is in our hearts. Without them, it is easy to become narcissistic as we learn about ourselves. It is easy to repeatedly look into the mirror and devalue or disregard the problem areas we are uncovering as well as place our mission, goals, and ambitions well above others we encounter.

We challenge you to be accountable to another human being for your actions and your choices. Until you are accountable and responsible for your own actions, you are not really prepared to either change or grow deeply. When we accept personal responsibility and accountability for our actions, we will begin to understand there is no one else responsible or to blame for our life situation; there is no hidden troll under life's bridge waiting to snatch us away from our journey. We are responsible for what we do, the choices we make, and how we interact with others in relationships.

Evaluating Your Progress

No goal setting, task development, or accountability program is complete without constant evaluation. Evaluation is a vital ingredient that brings our travel toward our personal mission statement full circle by making sure we are hitting the mark intended from the start. Evaluation assists in course correction before we get too far from our intentions. We (Becky and David) personally evaluate goal achievement and growth on a quarterly basis. This regular and consistent review reveals if we are on target or veering off course.

Utilizing members of your Personal Board of Directors or your accountability partner to assist you with your on-going evaluation is important. Provide for them a written copy of your goals and objectives, which grow out of your personal mission. Periodically, ask them, either collectively or individually, to help you determine what progress you are making. This part of the accountability process keeps your purpose-filled goals and fulfillment of your mission from being overpowered by life's daily and often demanding routines.

Becoming an Inspiration for Others to Follow

The process of discovery and mission development is not completed when you reach this section or have completed all the exercises we have included in the appendix. One final venture is necessary before proclaiming complete success. It is when we reproduce this success in others through challenge, encouragement, and example that our discovery is wholly complete. When we reach this maturity, we realize, almost instinctively, that we must help others in their own personal journey. As maturing people in the world of EI development, we are responsible for inviting others to take risks also, to become what they were created to be. Reaching this stage in life—termed *generativity*—helps us know it is worth the effort to assist others in experiencing fulfillment and meaning in life.[4]

The overarching concept explained throughout this book is captured in the word *metamorphosis.* This word provides an image that represents the most wondrous of transformations. It has come to signify how a thing totally changes in form, structure, and appearance over time (see Rom 12:1-2). The most eloquent representation throughout all history of this mysterious evolution is related to the butterfly. This delicate creation has come to represent new life, a refreshed spirit, beauty, and resurrection to new beginnings.

Thus, in a similar fashion, it can be with our own metamorphosis from our *Today-self* to the *Best-self* we are intended to become. We are born with most of the necessary ingredients for becoming emotionally intelligent. It is, however, a matter of whether we set in motion the transformation process by recognizing the need for discovering our gifts, strengths, and weaknesses, and how we might honor God through our lives.

Once we recognize our need for developing a healthy EI, we can begin applying the concepts of the *Best-self*. If we are persistent and willing to fill ourselves with good information and accurate assessment, we can begin to become a whole and healthy person (see Phil 4:8-9; Col 3:1-2).

Through reflection guided by mentors and coaches and through establishing goals, we take the steps necessary for closing the gaps that often exist between who we are and who we hope to be. We begin disassembling what holds us back from strengthening our EQ and actively becoming our *Best-self*. As we reflect and develop a healthy EI, we disassemble old selves and reassemble new attitudes and thought processes, which lead to habits that foster well-being across all areas of our lives (Eph 4:22-24; Col 3:12-14). It is this work that brings us to the threshold of complete metamorphosis—a transformation or change that we discover on purpose.

As authors, it is our hope you will not choose a life of cocooning, which is defined as "the practice of spending leisure time at home, especially watching television or using a VCR (or recording devices),"[5] but that you will heed the truth of this West African butterfly myth. There is no external makeover described in it, only the truth of what can happen when we undertake a deliberate journey of internal discovery and change.

> Two caterpillars were wandering through the tall grass looking for their favorite leaves when a beautiful butterfly fluttered overhead. One caterpillar was intrigued and in awe of the beautiful flying creature, while the other said that not for all the money in the world would he ever fly into the air like that. It was far too frightening. He felt that he belonged on the ground, safe and secure, with plenty of food, and that was where he was going to stay. The first caterpillar felt something stir in his heart when he saw the butterfly. He had an inner conviction that crawling on the ground was not his true nature. One day he would be up there, too, soaring with the birds and the butterflies.
>
> After some time of crawling and eating and yearning, the caterpillar changed into a beautiful butterfly with strong wings and many bright

colors, as he had dreamed all his life. But the other one stayed as he was, a caterpillar, crawling and eating leaves for the rest of his life because he never dared to dream or to know the meaning of his inner nature; he clung to what was familiar, what felt safe. He had no inkling of his true self. Only those who know their own true selves can soar like butterflies.[6]

Together, we have worked diligently to bring you into this moment. We have provided you with assessments and resources that will help you along the important journey of *Discovering You*. Additionally, we have offered you tools for closing the gap between what you are meant to be and who you are currently. We have done this through exposing you to the tools of goal setting, assessing how you utilize your time, and being accountable to someone else for your growth. We have provided tools for disassembling your current life and reassembling a life you were meant to live. We have done this because we believe it is God's highest good in how we live effectively in relationships by developing a healthy emotional intelligence. We have done this because we believe this book is an outgrowth of our own personal mission statements and what God has invited us, both individually and together, to be as disciples and people of faith.

The Moment of Truth

We cannot take you any further. Now, all we can do is remind you there is a choice that you will have to make—staying as you are at this moment or working at a lasting transformation that can reap peace and joy as you interact with others. From this intersection forward, it is your choice.

Over the course of our combined careers, we have encouraged hundreds of people to take this journey of discovery. Not all have made the choice to work diligently with this material when presented to them. Others have started the journey but stopped or became delayed when life got hard. Nevertheless, those who have worked diligently and consistently are renewed people, living full and fulfilling lives. They discovered a way of being that has allowed them to be all they were created to be. It is our prayer and trust in God that you will choose to join them in this adventure like no other.

EPILOGUE

We have personally experienced that this material changes one's life. We have taught the material contained in *Discovering You* individually and in partnership to hundreds of people since 2005. Repeatedly, unsolicited statements have come to us by those using the guide we provided in the previous sections. People have discovered who they are and what they are called to do in life, and begun implementing what they discerned. They have detected a purposeful place for their lives and found joy in the process of becoming what they were created to be.

The following are a few statements from those using this material. We know that what they express can also be your story if you choose to apply what you have discovered about yourself:

"I began studying the *Discovering You* workbook at a very pivotal time in my life. I was questioning my career path and searching for meaning and calling in my life. I have come through this process with a renewed sense of direction and have been awakened from an inauthentic and unpassionate life. I have a profoundly deeper understanding of who I am, who I want to be, and the changes I need to make to live life abundantly. I would highly recommend *Discovering You* to anyone who has a genuine interest in discovering their Best-self and living life with mission and purpose."

Melanie Peddicord, MBA, CPA, ABD
Professor of Accounting
Anderson University, Falls School of Business

"After completing the 360 feedback, understanding my real self and reflecting on my ideal self, it is clear to me that this *Discovering You* process is exactly what I needed to bring my ideal and real selves together. This process has already allowed me to get to know myself better and enable me to understand my self-awareness and self-management. I already have some great ideas for my personal growth plan and cannot wait to put it in writing."

Stephanie Ewing
MBA Student
Anderson University

We would be honored to add your story in a future edition of *Discovering You*. Contact us with your story. Until then, blessings, grace, and peace for each day of your life.

APPENDIX

Exercises, Inventories, and Recommended Readings

Appendix 1
GARDNER'S IDENTIFICATION OF MULTIPLE INTELLIGENCES

This matrix describes the types and descriptions of the multiple intelligences determined by Dr. Howard Gardner's research. For more detailed information and explanation, see his books cited in the endnotes. This matrix was created from the narrative in *Intelligence Reframed: Multiple Intelligences* (1999, 41-43, 47-66).

TYPE	DESCRIPTION
Linguistic Intelligence	"involves sensitivity to spoken and written language, the ability to learn languages, and the capacity to use language to accomplish certain goals. (Examples: lawyers, writers, speakers, and poets. Also, this has been highly valued by our current educational systems)"
Logical-mathematical Intelligence:	"involves the capacity to analyze problems logically, carry out mathematical operations, and investigate issues scientifically. (Examples: mathematicians, logicians, and scientists. These, too, are highly valued in our current educational systems)"
Musical Intelligence	"entails skill in the performance, composition, and appreciation of musical patterns. (Example: performing arts)"
Bodily-kinesthetic Intelligence	"entails the potential of using one's whole body or parts of the body (like the hand or mouth) to solve problems or fashion products. (Examples: dancers, actors, and athletes, but also craftspersons, surgeons, mechanics and other technically oriented professionals.)"
Spatial Intelligence	"features the potential to recognize and manipulate the patterns of wide space, as well as the patterns of more confined areas. (Examples: navigators, pilots, sculptors, surgeons, chess players, graphic artists, or architects.)"
Naturalist Intelligence	"denotes the ability to recognize, categorize, and classify species and characteristics of them. This entails the ability for recognizing the minutest of patterns through observation and perception. (Gardner notes that every culture values people who can recognize members of a species that are especially valuable or notably dangerous to our survival.)"
Existential Intelligence	"implies a concern with 'ultimate' issues; to engage in transcendental concerns, the spiritual realm. It must be noted that Gardner and his colleagues do not give this intelligence the same recognition as these listed above or the two remaining intelligences (he gives this intelligence a half rating), because it is the most difficult to understand and verify. But, as he notes, all cultures throughout humanity's history have valued those individuals who can convey an existential meaning to others (such as priests, pastors, shamans, and other religious thinkers)."
Intrapersonal Intelligence	"involves the capacity to understand oneself, to have an effective working model of oneself—including one's own desires, fears, and capacities—and to use such information effectively in regulating one's own life."
Interpersonal Intelligence	"denotes a person's capacity for understanding intentions, motivations, and desires of other people and consequently, to work effectively with others. Successful salespeople, teachers, clinicians, religious leaders, political leaders, and actors may possess these more acutely than others."

Appendix 2
360° FEEDBACK SHEETS INPUT FOR _____

(NAME OF PERSON BEING EVALUATED)

Instructions to the person completing this form: The person named above has a great desire and motivation to become an emotionally and relationally effective person. They have been working on a personal mission statement and identifying what they believe is their *Best-self.* This feedback will help them understand the gaps that may exist between their *Best-self* (who they believe they are) and what they currently display in their relationships with others (their *Today-self*). *Please be honest in how you respond.* Remember, the person listed above is asking for feedback that will help them become what they hope to be in all their relationships and work in the world. Return these sheets anonymously to the person within three days.

1. *How would you describe this person to others (e.g., fun, aggressive, optimistic, closed minded)?*

   _____

   _____

   _____

   _____

   _____

   _____

   _____

2. *What are this person's traits/behaviors that make them effective in relationship with you or others (e.g., talents, gifts, character traits, and behaviors)?*

   _____

   _____

   _____

   _____

   _____

   _____

   _____

3. *What are this person's traits/behaviors that make them less effective when being in relationship with you or others?*

_____

_____

_____

_____

_____

4. *What do you perceive as this individual's strongest talents, gifts, or character traits?*

_____

_____

_____

_____

_____

	The Person I am Evaluating....	Excellent 5 ————————➤	Satisfactory 3 ◄———		Poor ————— 1
1	*displays self-confidence in most situations*	5	4	3	2	1
2	*is optimistic, hopeful, and expects most things to turn out all right*	5	4	3	2	1
3	*is available and present with me when I need their help*	5	4	3	2	1
4	*gets along well with others and is sensitive to other cultures*	5	4	3	2	1
5	*is self-aware of their own strengths and weaknesses*	5	4	3	2	1
6	*is honest and trustworthy in their dealings with me*	5	4	3	2	1
7	*supports my dreams and interests*	5	4	3	2	1
8	*takes responsibility for mentoring and coaching others when needed or requested*	5	4	3	2	1
9	*easily understands and expresses their inner feelings*	5	4	3	2	1
10	*is a person of character that displays fairness, justice, and equity*	5	4	3	2	1
11	*seems interested in my personal welfare*	5	4	3	2	1

12	is open to dialogue when there is conflict; they are not defensive	5	4	3	2	1
13	appears to feel sure of themselves in most situations	5	4	3	2	1
14	remains clearheaded, calm, and controlled during stressful times	5	4	3	2	1
15	is empathic and patient in dealing with me and others	5	4	3	2	1
16	is comfortable in social settings and is enjoyable to be around	5	4	3	2	1
17	displays self-respect and is comfortable with who they are	5	4	3	2	1
18	displays control of impulses, emotions, and desires	5	4	3	2	1
19	listens to my needs	5	4	3	2	1
20	communicates well in all their relationships	5	4	3	2	1
21	seems to know what they are good at doing	5	4	3	2	1
22	is able to control anger effectively	5	4	3	2	1
23	enjoys helping others	5	4	3	2	1
24	values close relationships; makes friends easily	5	4	3	2	1
25	is aware of their own emotions and feelings	5	4	3	2	1
26	is adaptable when the situation demands this action	5	4	3	2	1
27	is sensitive to the needs of others	5	4	3	2	1
28	is assertive when needed and expresses opinions and feelings to others	5	4	3	2	1
29	is passionate about their interests	5	4	3	2	1
30	is willing to make short-term sacrifices for long-term improvement	5	4	3	2	1
31	is considerate and respectful of other people's feelings	5	4	3	2	1
32	is able to say "no" when appropriate to request of others	5	4	3	2	1

SCORING SHEET

Instructions

Step One: From the table below, notice how the questions are grouped for responses from your Feedback worksheet. Using the 360° feedback sheets you received from the individuals you contacted, post the scores from 5 to 1 for each statement number. If you had responses from more than individual, post all scores on this sheet and then add them together for each question and divide this total for each statement number by the number of responses received and place it in the "Your Scores & Avg." column. For example, if your respondents gave you a 3, 4, and 3 for statement one of "Self-Awareness," totals these numbers (10) and divide by 3 (3.33). Place this number in the "Your Avg. Score" column. Do this for all statements from the Feedback worksheets.

Step Two: After you have determined your scores for every category, total the columns. You will have a score for Self-Awareness, Self-Management, Social-Awareness, and Social Skills.

Self-Awareness		Self-Management	
Statement Number	**Your Avg. Score**	**Statement Number**	**Your Avg. Score**
1—self confidence		2—optimism	
5—self awareness		6—trust	
9—self awareness		10—trust	
13—self awareness		14—self-control and stress management	
17—self awareness		18—self control	
21—self awareness		22—self control	
25—self awareness		26—adaptable and flexible	
29—self awareness		30—self management	
Self-Awareness SCORE		**Self-Management SCORE**	

Social Awareness		Social Skills	
Statement Number	**Your Avg. Score**	**Statement Number**	**Your Avg. Score**
3—empathy		4—relationships	
7—empathy		8—development of others	

11—empathy		12—conflict management	
15—empathy		16—communication	
19—empathy		20—communication	
23—empathy		24—building bonds with others	
27—empathy		28—assertiveness	
31—empathy		32—assertiveness	
Social Awareness SCORE		**Social Skills SCORE**	

Step Three: Place your scores on the following graph; plot your total score for each area. Note the scores above 30; these represent your areas of strength. Scores below 30 identify potential gaps where you may desire to focus your efforts in order for you to become increasingly effective in your relationships.

Record a summary of your strengths and gaps on your Personal Growth Plan at the end of this workbook. Determine what goals you might add to your Personal Growth Plan that will assist you in becoming more effective in that area.

EI Area	Gap Areas						Strength Areas	
	5	10	15	20	25	30	35	40
Self-Awareness								
Self-Management								
Social Awareness								
Social Skills								

Appendix 3
TIME MANAGEMENT—DETERMINING PRIORITIES

The following activity will help you visually see how you are spending your time and will help you make conscious choices about the use of your days.

Step 1:

On the following pie chart, divide it proportionally by how you would typically spend the 24 hours you have each day. How you actually use your day is a reflection of your *Today-self.*

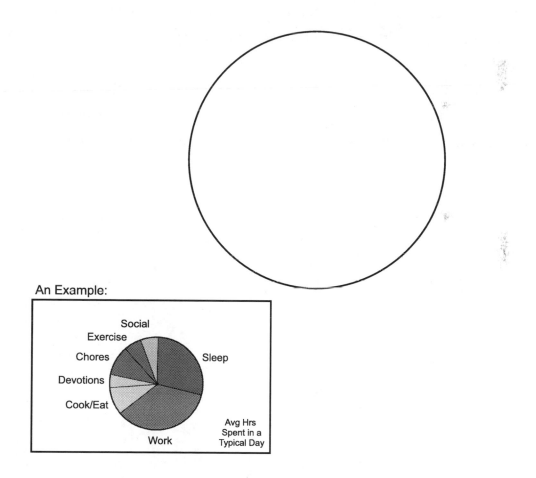

An Example:

Step 2:

Refer back to your work on your core values and personal mission statement (*Best-self*). What do they tell you about how you desire to use the time you have available? How would you use your time to live purposefully and with the priorities you believe important?

Step 3:

Identify the gaps between your *Best-self* and *Today-self* as reflected on your pie chart. What changes will help you be effective in the use of your time if it is to match your core values and personal mission statement?

Step 4:

Set a goal for beginning to give priority to those activities in life that are important to you. Set your calendar by these priorities first. Place all other appointments around these activities. You must schedule priorities just like any other appointment. If you do not, they will not be acted upon because they are not urgently screaming at you for completion. Remember this definition: a priority is "the supreme thing; the thing of greatest importance; the highest ranked thing of importance."

For example, if you need time weekly for reading, place an appointment on your calendar with yourself for reading. Treat this appointment as you would if someone was actually meeting with you. Don't break this appointment, even if you are tempted to do so.

Appendix 4
PERSONAL TIME BANDITS

We all have things in our lives that rob us of time. These bandits are uses of time that sap us of this tremendous resource. While we know that work activities and leisure are important, we also recognize that time can escape easily into many unproductive activities.

Sometimes bandits at work might be unfocused meetings, a cluttered desk, and decision traps like procrastination, the telephone, e-mail, undefined projects, or vague delegation. But also consider our time bandits at home, such as excessive computer use or endless hours of television, procrastination, and frittering away time just "hanging out doing nothing." Your time bandits are probably different from ours. But a personal self-examination will reveal yours to you.

In the following exercise, make a list of your personal time bandits that rob you of time on a daily basis. It is not enough to only name these bandits, but you must decide what to do about them in the future if you are to recapture proactive use of your time.

What are my Time Bandits at work:	How might I manage or better control these bandits?
What are my Time Bandits at home:	How might I manage or better control these bandits?
If I stop allowing these bandits to rob me, what will be the rewards?	

Learn to say no. This is one of the most vital tools of managing your time and gaining balance in your life. It is so simple, yet we get caught in the sense that there is an obligation for us to fill every moment with activity for some great cause. Learning to say no provides the time you might need for accomplishing what is vitally important and essential to you. Saying no can only happen when you know your priorities, have written goals and tasks, and are focused on making both areas realities.

We often believe time is an infinite resource. While time may be infinite, our use of it is finite. Wise use alone will determine our future circumstances. What choices will you make concerning the moments you have right now? Will you choose to use time in a way that brings satisfaction or will you squander the seconds? When your day is filled with busywork, procrastination, interruptions, time bandits, and other people's agendas, you naturally become stressed, distressed, burned-out, and unfocused. Your choices of how you manage your time will determine whether you will live in continual stress or with contentment.

Appendix 5
IDENTIFYING & OVERCOMING YOUR FEARS

One area that keeps us from focusing and growing or living with internal conflict is how we deal with our fears—whether fear of failure or fear of success. In this exercise related to goal attainment, we encourage you to address those things that are holding you back, fears that are keeping you from moving forward in life, even though you want to break free and fly. As with other segments of this transformation process, we encourage you to provide this information to an accountability partner or coach in order for you to reach what you believe is your *Best-self.*

Begin this exercise with the following question then complete the boxes below:

"What keeps you from living out your personal mission and life calling? Anything? What barriers or fears (like failure, rejection, etc.) might be holding you back from achieving what you are called to be and do in life?"

Make a list of the barriers or things that hold you back:	
What is the worst that could happen to you if your fears came true?	
What is the likelihood of these things happening? (from the above box)	
If you take the necessary risks to live your dreams, life calling, or personal mission, what are the rewards for you and others? List the potential benefits for you and others?	

Appendix 6
STRESSORS—GNAWING SENSE OF ANXIETY (GSA)

This exercise is similar to the activity of identifying your fears. While this activity does not name additional fears, it does identify those things that cause you stress or keep you from remaining focused. Your GSA refers to our "Gnawing Sense of Anxiety," a phrase coined by management consultant David Allen. Our stressors, Allen believes, come not from having a lot to do or accomplish, but from not keeping our agreements or promises with ourselves; for not completing what we agreed to do. For example, have you ever made a New Year's resolution that you did not keep? And in time, did you begin to feel guilty about not keeping this resolution? Probably. With this passing of time, you begin saying things like, "I just can't do it, but I know I should." Or, "I have tried to do this a hundred times; I guess I just don't have what it takes to make it happen." It is just a matter of time before you are down on yourself, heaping on negative self-talk, or becoming more frustrated each time you think of that activity or promise you made.

Identifying the Stressors (or Incompletes) in Your Life
Make a list of all the things you have promised yourself you would do (e.g., lose weight, clean out the garage, finish your degree) but still have not completed or even attempted. **Be as exhaustive as possible in creating and compiling this list of stressors (or incompletes).** This activity was created based on Allen's 1998 premise.[1]

Step 1: Go through the list and think how these uncompleted tasks make you feel.

Step 2: Go through the list again, crossing off all those things you will honestly never do or undertake. Be honest and don't agonize over crossing them off. For example, if you are never going to clean out the garage, cross if off the list and forget it.

Step 3: From the remaining items on the list, circle all the things you will complete or undertake **in the next two weeks**. Be realistic in what you can do in the time you have.

Step 4: Finally, write out all the things that you will complete **in the next six months** because they are large projects. Again, be realistic. Work these into your goals, giving them specific date and time measurements as you have with other goals. This is essential if you desire to get closer to your *Best-self* in the process of rearranging your life on purpose.

Appendix 7
ACCOUNTABILITY PARTNERS, COACHES, AND MENTORS

Accountability Partners

We need others to hold us accountable for maturing and growing toward a life demonstrated by a strong EI. *Accountability Partners* are people we fully trust with confidentiality who will help us remain focused and accountable for our actions and progress. Developing and growing can happen individually, in private, but one cannot be catapulted forward if there is no accountability for our growth.

An accountability partner will help you more fully understand yourself through regular conversation. What do you long to quench in your soul that you will need assistance to resolve? What action steps have you planned or are planning that will require that someone ask you about your progress on a regular basis? Your accountability partner will serve as this person for making sure you are staying focused and working on the gap areas between your *Best-self* and your *Today-self.*

We offer some suggestions from our own personal experiences and development from having accountability partners. At the forefront, we must throw out a few signposts for taking this path seriously: ***"Be Cautious," "Be Weary," and "Be Sure of Those Whom You Choose to Guide You."*** It is essential to heed these warnings because having an accountability partner places you in one of the most vulnerable aspects of your life. In the work with an accountability partner, you are exposing your most inner being, your life force, your spirit, and your very breath of life to another person. Having a person at this deep level giving spiritual, life-altering guidance who has ulterior motives, need for control, or their own personal demons can mortally wound you. So, one last measure in this tune: ***"Be Watchful."***

Now, having piped that cautionary chorus, let us share some steps you might consider in locating and entering into a relationship that can strengthen your EI. From the outset, you must be serious about this enterprise, because it can extract the most exhilarating and exhausting emotions of your life. The first step is that you know something about yourself before you seek an accountability partner. The next step is selecting an accountability partner. The use of the partner word is intentional. You must also remember *this person is NOT a counselor or therapist.* You are engaged with them to help you grow and develop in this most vital segment of your life. This journey is not simply about empty pail learning—that is having someone fill you up with their wisdom—but a partnership. This is always important to keep in mind. If they become the advice giver and you the receiver, then the partnership may become one sided, not truly fulfilling its intended purpose of helping you with this personal metamorphosis. Logistically, then, consider several persons whom you might approach about this partnership. They must be willing and have time for you. They are, in a sense, accountable to you and for your development. *So consider this individual wisely.*

Our advice would also be that the person is of the same gender. This advice simply stems from the reality that as you share together, conversation can become more intimate. As we noted earlier, if the person you choose does not have a sound personal ethic or understand boundaries, they can take advantage of you.

It might be useful to also have either a verbal or written agreement as to the mutual accountability between each of you. It might cover the duration of your time together, what you might discuss together, what books you might read together, or other matters of importance to you. This agreement can serve as the boundary that is needed between both of you so that your partner does not overtly become the dominant truth-giver in the exchange, but does allow you to develop through a healthy give and take.

As a final step, you need to determine when and how you will evaluate your growth. Are you experiencing and can you verbalize growth in your life? How is that growth being reflected outwardly and inwardly? Journal writing along this transformation, noting your feelings, questions, answers and growth, might serve as a valuable tool in this evaluation.

Personal or Executive Coach

The use of a coach is increasing in popularity with many individuals and in many organizations. Coaches differ from an accountability partner due to their qualifications or certifications through a recognized coaching school. Coaching training provides them with the tools for assisting individuals in personal growth and development. Coaching may involve expanding a skill, modifying a behavior, or assisting an individual with shifting a paradigm that is holding them back in their life and relationships.

A coach does not need to be an expert in your field of work. Additionally, coaching should not involve following a packaged model or prescribed approach. The coach is involved with you personally as you strive to become more effective in your personal or professional life. The role of the coach is to provide objective assessment and observations for increasing your self-awareness. The coach should challenge your hidden areas, reveal fresh perspectives, and encourage you to follow an action plan for addressing personal issues and forming new habits. The action plan should be tailored to your unique dreams and aspirations.

It is also important to note your own personal role in making a coaching relationship successful. You must first be motivated to change and accept personal responsibility for carrying out suggested action plans for growth. It is important to communicate aspirations and expectations, to jointly agree on a coaching agenda, and to plan for when to end the relationship.

A personal or executive coach is not a consultant who is paid to tell the client what to do. A coach is not a therapist who deals with mental illness and emotional issues of the past. Coaches focus their efforts on assisting highly functional, successful people with balancing their lives and effectively implementing new skills and behaviors.

Mentor

A mentoring relationship differs from both accountability partners and coaching in that a mentor is usually someone who is experienced in your specific industry or career area. Some organizations routinely team up a less experienced employee with a higher-ranking mentor. The mentor shares wisdom and advice concerning the particular organization. Unlike a coach, a mentor is usually not paid a fee for services. Mentoring is commonly included in the job descriptions of managers as they fulfill their responsibility for developing their employees and helping them identify their shadow areas. Regular attention will provide the needed energy for breaking away or at least having self-control over these life areas.

SELF-AWARENESS PROFILE DETAILED WORKSHEEET

(You may use this to record your reflections—or the one page Self-Awareness Profile summary sheet)

Name: _____   Initial Date Completed: _____

My BEST-SELF: What I hope to become or leave behind (thoughts from Step One)

My passion and dreams are:

_____
_____
_____
_____
_____
_____

The legacies I want to leave are:

_____
_____
_____
_____
_____
_____

My core values are:

_____
_____
_____
_____
_____
_____

My personal mission statement is:

_____

_____

_____

My TODAY-SELF: My assessment of where I am at this point in my life (observations and responses from Step Three)

360-Degree Feedback from others

My strengths are:

_____

_____

_____

_____

Gaps or areas for improvement that are needed:

_____

_____

_____

_____

EQ Self-Report

My strengths are:

_____

_____

_____

_____

Gaps or areas for improvement that are needed:

_____

_____

_____

_____

Self-awareness insights from other inventories (such as Learning Styles, MBTI, Spiritual Gifts)

My strengths are:

_____

_____

_____

_____

Gaps or areas for improvement that are needed:

_____

_____

_____

_____

Other notes or personal insights:

_____

_____

_____

_____

SELF-AWARENESS PROFILE

Name:_____   **Date Completed:**_____

Step One: BEST-SELF

Step One: <u>Passion/Dreams:</u>

Step Two: <u>Legacy Themes:</u>

Step Three: <u>Core Values:</u>

Step Four: <u>Personal Mission Statement:</u>

Step Two: TODAY-SELF

<u>360° Feedback from Others:</u>
Strengths—

Gaps—

<u>EQ Self Report:</u>
Strengths—

Gaps—

<u>MBTI:</u> Type __ __ __ __
Strengths—

Gaps—

<u>Learning Style:</u>

<u>Spiritual Gifts (or other assessments):</u>

Note: Use this sheet for logging summary comments from your completed exercises and assessments. This will be a useful reference when developing your Personal Growth Plan.

PERSONAL GROWTH PLAN

My personal mission statement is:

_____

_____

_____

From my personal mission statement, I am setting the following goals. These goals will specifically develop my identified strengths as noted in my assessments and will also help me become more effective in areas or gaps between my *Best-self* and *Today-self*. (It is valuable to consider all aspects of your life when setting goals: professional, personal, spiritual, physical, etc.)

Date these Goals were written:	Target Date	Completed
GOAL:		
ACTION STEPS: 1. 2. 3. 4.		
GOAL:		
ACTION STEPS: 1. 2. 3. 4.		

Date these Goals were written:	Target Date	Completed
GOAL:		
ACTION STEPS: 1. 2. 3. 4.		
GOAL:		
ACTION STEPS: 1. 2. 3. 4.		

RECOMMENDED READINGS FOR FURTHER STUDY

Books. There are so many books in the world. So much reading, so much time spent in trying to gather it all in. And yet we need books and thoughts for stimulating our thinking, guiding us, distressing us in some way that will lead us to living with greater satisfaction, and helping us through the transformation process into what we are intended to be during life.

We recommend the following books related to the development of specific areas of EI. We have read them all and believe they will give you additional insights and challenges toward that personal metamorphosis that we have offered to you throughout this workbook. We hope you will read them, write in them, and allow them to lead you into a deeper understanding of yourself and the legacies you are preparing throughout your life's pilgrimage. We guarantee they will be like an ice pick breaking the frozen sea inside you.

Emotional Intelligence Overall

Boyatzis, Richard, and Annie McKee. *Resonant Leadership*. Boston: Harvard Business Press, 2005.

Goleman, Daniel. *Emotional Intelligence: Why It Can Matter More Than IQ*. New York: Bantam, 2006.

Nelson, Darwin, and Gary Low. *Emotional Intelligence: Achieving Academic and Career Excellence*. Boston: Prentice Hall, 2011.

Stein, Steven. *The 7 Keys to an Emotionally Intelligent Organization*. San Francisco: Jossey-Bass, 2007.

Stein, Steven, and Howard Book. *The EQ Edge: Emotional Intelligence and Your Success*. Toronto: Multi-Health Systems, Inc., 2000.

Stock, Byron. *Smart Emotions for Busy Business People*. St. Joseph, MI: Byron Stock & Associates LLC, 2008

Self-Awareness

Bradberry, Travis. *The Personality Code*. New York: The Penguin Group, 2007.

Buckingham, Marcus, and Donald O. Clifton. *Now, Discover Your Strengths*. New York: Free Press, 2001.

Eldredge, John. *Dare to Desire: An Invitation to Fulfill Your Deepest Dreams.* Nashville, TN: Thomas Nelson, 2002.

Frankl, Viktor. *Man's Search for Meaning*. 4th edition. Boston: Beacon Press, 1992.

Goleman, Daniel, Richard Boyatzis, and Annie McKee. *Primal Leadership: Learning to Lead with Emotional Intelligence*, Boston: Harvard Business School Press, 2002.

Manning, Brennan. *Abba's Child: The Cry of the Heart for Intimate Belonging*. Colorado Springs, CO: NavPress, 1999

McCarthy, Kevin W. *The On-Purpose Business: Doing More of What You Do Best More Profitably*. Colorado Springs, CO: Pinon Press, 1998.

Neidert, David. *Four Seasons of Leadership: Creating and Sustaining Personal Leadership and Life Legacies*. Bloomington, IN: Unlimited Publishing, 2008.

Oswald, Roy, Arland Johnson, and Loren Mead. *The Emotional Intelligence of Jesus: Relational Smarts for Religious Leaders*. Lanham, MD: Rowman & Littlefield Publishers, 2015.

Palmer, Parker. *Let Your Life Speak: Listening for the Voice of Vocation*. San Francisco: Jossey-Bass Publishers, 2000.

Palmer, Parker. *A Hidden Wholeness: The Journey Toward an Undivided Life*. San Francisco: Jossey-Bass Publishers, 2004.

Sinek, Simon. *Start with Why: How Great Leaders Inspire Everyone to Take Action*. New York: Portfolio/Penguin, 2011.

Sternberg, Robert. *Successful Intelligence*. New York: Simon & Schuster, 1996.

Warren, Rick. *The Purpose-Driven Life: What on Earth Am I Here For?* Grand Rapids, MI: Zondervan Publishing Company, 2002.

Self-Management

Canfield, Jack, Mark Victor Hansen, and Les Hewitt. *The Power of Focus: How to Hit Your Business, Personal and Financial Targets with Absolute Certainty*. Deerfield, FL: Health Communications, 2000.

Covey, Stephen. *Seven Habits of Highly Effective People*. New York: Simon & Schuster, 1989.

Covey, Stephen, Roger Merrill, and Rebecca Merrill. *First Things First*. New York: Simon & Schuster, 2004.

Johnson, Spencer. *Who Moved My Cheese?* New York: G.P. Putnam's Sons, 1998.

Livingston, Scott. *Seven Secrets of an Emotionally Intelligent Coach*. Noblesville, IN: Buttermilk Ridge Publishing, 2007.

Lundin, Stephen C., Harry Paul, and John Christensen. *Fish! A Remarkable Way to Boost Morale and Improve Results.* New York: Hyperion, 2000.

McGinniss, Alan Joy. *The Power of Optimism*. New York: Harper & Row Publishers, 1990.

Paulus, Trina. *Hope for the Flowers*. New York: Paulist Press, 1972.

Scazzero, Peter. *Emotionally Healthy Spirituality: It's Impossible to Be Spiritually Mature, While Remaining Emotionally Immature*. Grand Rapids, MI: Zondervan, 2014.

Segal, Jeanne. *Raising Your Emotional Intelligence: A Hands-on Program for Harnessing the Power of Your Instincts and Emotions.* Owl Books, 1997.

Seligman, Martin E. P. *Learned Optimism: How to Change Your Mind and Your Life.* New York: Alfred A. Knopf, 1990.

Social Awareness

Albom, Mitch. *Tuesdays with Morrie: An Old Man, a Young Man, and Life's Greatest Lessons.* New York: Broadway Books, 1998.

Berens, Linda. *Quick Guide to the 16 Personality Types in Organizations: Understanding Personality Differences in the Workplace.* Huntington Beach, CA: Telos Publications, 2001.

Bonhoeffer, Dietrich. *Life Together.* New York: Harper Collins, 1954.

Bowling, John. *A Way With Words.* Kansas City, MO: Beacon Hill Press of Kansas City, 1999.

Merton, Thomas. *No Man is an Island.* New York: Harvest Books, 1955.

Pearman, Roger. *Introduction to Type and Emotional Intelligence.* Palo Alto, CA: CPP, Inc., 2002.

Spears, Larry (ed). *Insights on Leadership: Service, Stewardship, Spirit and Servant Leadership.* New York: John Wiley & Sons, 1997.

Social Skills

Blanchard, Ken. *Gung Ho! Turn On the People in Any Organization.* New York: William Morrow, 1997.

Blanchard, Ken, and Don Shula. *Everyone's A Coach.* New York: Harper Business/ Zondervan, 1995.

Chapman, Gary. *The Five Love Languages: How to Express Heartfelt Commitment to Your Mate*. Chicago, IL: Moody Publishers, 1996.

Collins, Jim. *Good to Great: Why Some Companies Make the Leap... and Others Don't*. New York: Collins, 2001.

Dungy, Tony. *The Mentor Leader: Secrets of Building People and Teams That Win Consistently*. Carol Stream, IL: Tyndale House Publishers, 2010.

Patterson, Kerry, Joseph Grenny, Ron McMillan, Al Switzler, and Stephen R. Covey. *Crucial Conversations: Tools for Talking When Stakes Are High*. New York, NY: McGraw-Hill, 2002.

ENDNOTES

Foreword

1 All scripture references are from the Today's New International Version, Zondervan, Grand Rapids, MI, 2005.

2 James Long, "Peter Scazzero: Emotionally Healthy Leadership, An Interview," *Outreach Magazine*, Sept/Oct 2015, 76.

Introduction

1 Long, "Peter Scazzero," 70.

2 Job Outlook Report of 2009.

3 George E. Vaillant, *Aging Well: Surprising Guideposts to a Happier Life from the Landmark Harvard Study of Adult Development* (New York: Little, Brown and Company, 2003). Note that emotional intelligence (EI) is measured by emotional quotient (EQ) in matters focusing on this developmental area.

4 Ibid., 26, 97. Cary Cherniss and Daniel Goleman report EI begins developing early in life. Our experiences shape our brain patterns and these habitual patterns reinforce how we consider new developments. (Cary Cherniss and Daniel Goleman, "Bringing Emotional Intelligence to the Workplace," *The Consortium for Research on Emotional Intelligence in Organizations*, summary report, 1998, 5.)

5 Richard Boyatzis notes there are three clusters of competencies, i.e., cognitive (thinking patterns), EI, and social (cultural). He writes these competencies can be developed creating behavioral change in each of the areas. Boyatzis defines competencies as the capacity or ability (behaviors) organized around an intended use. To gain understanding in each, we need to listen, think, read, ask questions, engage in different experiences, and more. (Richard Boyatzis, "Competencies in the 21st Century," *Journal of Management Development*, 2008, 6, 7, 10.

6 The New Testament, particularly Paul's letters, remind us we are in partnership with God through his Spirit to change. We encourage the reader to study closely Ephesians 4:17-5:20 and Paul's admonition to put off old ways and "be made new in the attitude of your minds" (Eph 4:23).

7 One of the most insightful books we recommend is *A Hidden Wholeness: The Journey Toward an Undivided Life*, by Parker Palmer (Jossey-Bass Publishers, 2004). The subtitle of the book is "Welcoming the Soul and Weaving Community in a Wounded World." In the book, Palmer reminds us that many live divided lives, i.e., we live one way daily, but our hearts ache for something we know is whispering to us from the deepest places of our being. The book challenges the reader to utilize circles of trust to help identify what is at the deepest part of our being. In our book, we suggest the activity of the board of directors, which can led you to deeper self-awareness.

8 EQ scholars use a variety of terms for this idea. Some use *authentic self*; others use *ideal* and *real self*. We have chosen to use the terms *Best* and *Today*. Best-self is what we believe you were created to become. The purpose is what we are helping you to identify and clarify in this material. *Today-self* is how you are today. We use these terms because all this material has a movement theme underlying

what we share and suggest. It is a movement from today to tomorrow, from Today to the Best you hope to achieve.

9   Long, "Peter Scazzero," 73.

10   Ibid.

11   Daniel Goleman, *Emotional Intelligence: Why It Can Matter More Than IQ* (Bantam Books, 1995). Goleman notes in his book that being a better learner, being happier, and being healthier are benefits of EI (pp. 68, 85, 168).

12   Travis Bradbury, bestselling author and cofounder of TalentSmart, states that emotionally intelligent people tend to have a "robust emotional vocabulary." By this he means people have an "extensive vocabulary of feelings" where they may not say they are feeling "bad," but "can pinpoint whether they are 'irritable,' 'frustrated,' 'downtrodden,' or 'anxious.'" "The more specific your word choice, the better insight you have into exactly how you are feeling, what caused it, and what you should do about it." (Travis Bradbury, "18 signs you have high emotional intelligence," Business Insider.com, February 19, 2015. Accessed August 31, 2015. www.businessinsider.com/18-signs-you-have-high-emotional-intelligence.)

Exploring Emotional Intelligence

1   Martin Seligman's most recent book shows the link between EQ concepts and overall happiness in life. It is a good resource and support for the task of developing over your lifetime. Martin F.P. Seligman, *Flourish: A Visionary New Understanding of Happiness and Well-Being*, (New York: Free Press, 2011).

2   Kate Cannon, one of the first trainers to apply EQ widely at American Express, shares the definition used by John Mayer and Peter Salovey (two early researchers in EI) in her book ebook, *Building Your Capacity 2 Change*, to expand the definition of EI. Mayer and Salovey define EI as "monitoring the feelings of yourself and others to discriminate among them and use that understanding for guiding thinking and actions." The process as presented by Mayer and Salovey is like the branch of a tree: *Perceiving* emotions (a fundamental skill) leads to *Using* those insights (for thinking, problem solving, and decision making). This leads to *Understanding* (emotional language and the complexity of emotions) and finally to *Managing* emotions (i.e., regulating our personal emotions and using this to influence others for good or to at least be aware of our or other's potential darker motives). (Kate Cannon, *Building Your Capacity 2 Change* [ebook, 2008], 14.)

3   Long, "Peter Scazzero," 69. Scazzero goes on to say in this interview that emotionally healthy leaders "have a significant emotional awareness-they face their shadows. They know their good sides and their ugly sides, and how they impact their leadership. They have slowed down their lives to have a deep walk with God out of which they lead. And they've got some rhythms in their life-how they work and how they Sabbath-so that their life isn't all work but has a biblical rhythm to it."

4   Travis Bradbury's terminology is also melded into this matrix. (Travis Bradberry, "Why You Need Emotional Intelligence to Succeed," *Forbes*, January 7, 2015. www.forbes.com/sites/travisbradberry/2015/01/07/why-you-need-emotional-intelligence-to-succeed. Accessed August 30, 2015.

5   Steven B. Wolff, *Emotional Competence Inventory (ECI): Technical Manual* (Hay Group, McClelland Center for Research and Innovation: 2005). http://www.eiconsortium.org/pdf/ECI_2_0_Technical_Manual_v2.pdf (Accessed August 2015).

6   The EQ-i 2.0 Mode and Science Behind It. MHS Assessments. https://tap.mhs.com/EQi20TheScience.aspx (Accessed August 2015).

7   The concept of multiple intelligences is used in this material as postulated by Dr. Howard Gardner, a pioneer and expert in this field. For more extensive understanding, see his books *Intelligence Reframed: Multiple Intelligence for the 21st Century* (1999), *Multiple Intelligences: New Horizons in Theories and Practice* (1993), Frames *of Mind: The Theories of Multiple Intelligences* (1983), and *Mind of the Future* (2011).

8   Howard Gardner, *Multiple Intelligences* (New York: Basic Books,1993), 43

9   Cherniss and Goleman, "Bringing Emotional Intelligence to the Workplace," 6-7, 14. The authors remind us we cannot unlearn behaviors in one seminar. There must be a motivation to learn, which comes via assessment. This assessment helps identify what is needed for the step of learning. Learning comes via training or being connected to a trainer. The relationship of the trainer and trainee is critical. There must be empathy, trust, clear goals for the learning environment, and frequent feedback. Learning can then be transferred to actual activity where individuals ask, "How will I use what I have learned in this week?" This final step is then evaluated within the context of desiring to grow and learn about oneself.

10 Filmmaker Luke Renner has been exploring this invitation in his film *The T Word: Trauma*. This documentary chronicles the lives of many people who had horrific experiences in their lives but choose not to be defined by them. These everyday people have chosen hope in the midst of despair. This film began production during 2014.

11 Morris Massey, 1990 Keynote address, International Management Council of the YMCA National Conference. Massey also coined the phrase "significant emotional events" (SEE) which implies that a person will not change their present circumstances unless a SEE like health, loss of job, death, etc. forces one to consider their situation. The Greeks called this *askesis*, a voluntary examination of one's life.

12 We encourage you to read books from the recommended reading section in the appendix to understand the scientific background of EI and the research that serves as a foundation for this book.

Step One

1   Daniel Goleman, Richard Boyatzis, and Annie McKee, *Primal Leadership: Learning to Lead with Emotional Intelligence* (Cambridge, MA: Harvard Business School Press, 2002).

2   Parker Palmer, *Let Your Life Speak: Listening for the Voice of Vocation* (San Francisco: Jossey-Bass Publishers, 2000), 3.

3   Po Bronson, *What Should I Do with My Life?: The True Story of People Who Answered the Ultimate Question*, (New York: Ballantine Books, 2005), jacket flap.

4   Long, "Peter Scazzero," 73.

5   Kim Williams and Doug Johnson, "Three Wooden Crosses," *Rise and Shine* (Word Music: TX), 2005.

6   http://www.teamtechnology.co.uk/personality/types/enfp/careers/

7   Stephen R. Covey, A. Roger Merrill, and Rebecca Merrill, *First Things First*, (New York: Free Press, 1995), 82.

8   Most of these values words come from a 1999 study conducted by the Centers for Ethical Leadership. They also provide this Core Values Assessment for Individuals in a download. www.ethicalleadership.org

9   David's mission statement evolved over time. He was searching for a word that brought it all together. Over many years, he tried a variety of phrases, but none of them brought clarity or a sense of fulfilling God's purpose for his life. On a Sunday morning at the end of the worship service, he watched people move to the front of the church at the end of the sermon. It was then he believes the Holy Spirit spoke and gave the word *invitation*. David's mission phrase now begins with "inviting" because that is what God does—invites. The remaining part of his mission statement, "being and doing good," is directly connected to Peter's sermon in Acts 10:38, "and how he [Jesus] went around doing good." The Greek word captures the beneficial effect of life for others. This mission grew in time from a full English sentence to seven words: Inviting people to be and do good. Through this statement, David believes he is following the model of Jesus as preached by Peter. Thus as God invites and we choose, so David can only invite and people will make a choice to discover what God intends for them.

10   Laura Beth Jones, *The Path*, (New York: Hyperion, 1996).

11   We often discount personal retreats or solitude as a waste of our time. However, if we pay attention to some of the greatest literature in the world, some written centuries ago, many of the authors advocate for solitude and retreat. This is the heart of spiritual formation and renewal. One of the leading advocates for soul care today is Parker Palmer, who is also helping give clarity to the work of emotional intelligence.

Step Two

1   Goleman, Boyatzis, and McKee, *Primal Leadership*, 135.

2   Palmer, *Let Your Life Speak*, 6.

3   Long, "Peter Scazzero," 73.

4   The Critical Thinking Institute at the University of California, Berkley, reminds us that as people we are easily self delusional when it comes to acknowledging what is really happening internally and what we believe about ourselves. It is easy to justify our behaviors and thoughts when we are the only one assessing them.

5   Gene Wilkes, Discover Your Spiritual Gifts! Spiritual Gifts Survey. Lifeway Christian Resources. http://www.lifeway.com/lwc/files/lwcf_pdf_discover_your_spiritual_gifts.pdf (Accessed August 2015).

Step Three

1   Goleman, Boyatzis, and McKee, *Primal Leadership*, 116.

2   Research by Richard Boyatizis determined that setting positive goals is important as goals "open us up to new opportunities." Positive goal setting focuses on strengths as well as helping us maintain joy in both practice and learning. (Daniel Goleman, "The Power of Positive Planning," LinkedIn, www.linkedin.com/today/post/article/20140528163448-117825785-the-power-of-positive-planning. Accessed May 28, 2014.)

3   We highly recommend a number of books for understanding the power of goal setting. These books not only describe goal setting but why it is essential for living successfully: Brian Tracy, *Goals!: How to Get Everything You Want—Faster Than You Ever Thought Possible* (New York: Berrett-Koehler Publishers, 2010); David Allen, *Getting Things Done: The Art of Stress-Free Productivity* (New York: Penguin Books, 2002). Also, Parker Palmer, in his book *The Hidden Wholeness*, gives example after example, of times when working with teachers, that show trusting another person to help and listen to you is essential in personal development.

4   Generativity is a stage identified by Vaillant in the Harvard study on successful aging. People who reach this stage in life actually live in peace as they encourage others through the example of their own lives. See George E. Vaillant, *Aging Well: Surprising Guideposts to a Happier Life from the Landmark Harvard Study of Adult Development* (New York: Little, Brown and Company, 2003).

5   Dictionary.com, http://dictionary.reference.com/browse/cocooning (Accessed July 6, 2014).

6   Maraleen Manos-Jones, *The Spirit of Butterflies: Myth, Magic and Art* (New York: Harry N. Abrams, 2000), 123.

Appendix 6

1   Don't Manage Time, Manage Yourself, David Beardsley 03.31.98.
    http://www.fastcompany.com/33961/dont-manage-time-manage-yourself

Rebecca Haskett, EdD, is currently professor of business management at Anderson University's Falls School of Business, teaching in the areas of management, organizational behavior, nonprofit leadership, and strategic planning. She has been on the faculty since 1996. She completed her EdD in higher education at Indiana University, with a minor in nonprofit strategic management. Haskett's doctoral dissertation is *Emotional Intelligence and Teaching Success in Higher Education.*

Rebecca is the co-founder of the EQ "Think Tank" networking organization. She is a certified trainer in TalentSmart Emotional Intelligence training curriculum and the Emotional Intelligence Appraisal, and has completed the BarOn EQ-i Emotional Intelligence Certification program. She also presents seminars and workshops on EI. Some of her recent clients include the Department of Homeland Security, Edward Jones, Indiana Business College, and Center for Mental Health, as well as Ball State University as a keynote speaker on topic of EI for their annual Teaching and Learning Conference.

Rebecca's past experience includes 17 years as a CPA for General Motors, along with leading the organizational strategic planning process. She may be contacted at bahaskett@anderson.edu.

David Neidert, MA, is the author of the nationally distributed book *Four Seasons of Leadership*, now in its third edition (Unlimited Publishing, 2008). Additionally, he has contributed to the book *A New Paradigm of Leadership: A Vision of Excellence for 21st Century Organizations*, with authors such as Stephen Covey, Ken Blanchard, Peter Senge, and Peter Drucker (1997). He also is a contributor, with his daughter, to the book *Love: Bridges of Reconciliation* (2003). He has edited nearly a dozen curricular manuals as well as authored others used nationally for theological and biblical studies. His first children's book is *God Quest: Search*Explore*Discover* (Warner Press, Inc., July 2007).

David has been teaching at the university level since 1987 and has also taught more than 200 seminars and workshops across the country. He is a former national president of the International Management Council of the YMCA (IMC) and former chair of the Board of Regents of the Institute of Certified Professional Managers (an international management certification and testing institute) at James Madison University, Harrisonburg, Virginia, and past chair of the Board of Directors, Indiana Ministries of the Church of God. He has also been trained by the Center for Creative Leadership (Greensboro, NC).

David has received a variety of awards for his civic involvement and teaching, including IMC's highest honor, The 2003 Wilbur McFeely Award, for his books and teaching in the area of human development and leadership. He served with Anderson University from 1978 to 2016 in a variety of capacities, including director of human resources, director of auxiliary services, and the director of admissions and enrollment coordinator, the graduate School of Theology. He is currently a professional speaker, writer, and consultant. He may be contacted at *dlneidert@anderson.edu*.

Printed in the United States
By Bookmasters